Collins Children's Pictorial Atlas
Collins
An imprint of HarperCollins Publishers
77-85 Fulham Palace Road
London
W6 8JB

© 2007 by HarperCollins Publishers Ltd
Maps © Collins Bartholomew Ltd 2007

This 2009 edition published by Sandy Creek,
by arrangement with HarperCollins Publishers.

All mapping in this atlas is generated from Collins Bartholomew™ digital
databases. Collins Bartholomew™, the UK's leading independent
geographical information supplier, can provide a digital, custom, and
premium mapping service to a variety of markets.
For further information:
e-mail: collinsbartholomew@harpercollins.co.uk
Visit our website at: www.collinsbartholomew.com

Sandy Creek
122 Fifth Avenue
New York, NY 10011

ISBN: 978-1-4351-1999-4

Printed and bound in Singapore

10 9 8 7 6 5 4 3 2 1

*The contents of this edition of the Collins Children's Pictorial Atlas
are believed correct at the time of printing. Nevertheless the publishers
can accept no responsibility for errors or omissions, changes in detail
given, or for any expense or loss thereby caused.*

Collins
Children's
Pictorial Atlas

Sandy Creek

Contents

iv-v   How to use the atlas

vi-vii   World Interesting places

viii-ix   World Animals and birds

x-xi   World Food and drink

xii-xiii   World Sports and activities

xiv-xv   World Natural features

xvi-xvii   World Countries and cities

North America   2

Canada   4

United States of America   6

Mexico and the Caribbean   8

South America   10

South America North   12

South America South   14

Africa   16

Northern Africa   18

Southern Africa   20

Europe   22

United Kingdom and Ireland   24

Northern Europe   26

Southern Europe   28

Asia   30

Russian Federation   32

Southwest Asia   34

South Asia   36

China and Japan   38

Southeast Asia   40

Oceania   42

Australia and New Zealand   44

The Arctic Ocean   46

Antarctica   47

Where have you been?   48
What do you think?

Countries of the world   52

Games and Quizzes   56

Index   60

How to use the atlas

Take a journey around the world with this atlas. It is divided up into continents, regions and countries. Each map is full of small picture symbols which will introduce you to the lifestyle of people, wildlife and interesting places found in far off lands.

World maps

The introductory pages show maps of the whole world and from these you can find the regions with the most interesting features. You can find out more about these by searching through the continents and regions mapped in the rest of the atlas. At the bottom of each World page is a list of symbols used on pages within the atlas. Try to find the countries where the symbols are shown then look at the other interesting features found in that country.

Below the world map each 'Did you know? lists some fascinating facts and statistics.

- Only 12 people have ever walked on the moon.
- It takes 45 minutes to put on a space suit.
- A spacecraft takes 3 days to travel from earth to the moon.

World

The world is full of interesting places. Many countries have famous buildings like castles, churches and palaces and some of these are named on the map.

NORTH AMERICA

Seattle Space Needle

Statue of Liberty

Kennedy Space Center

Mexican pyramid

Arctic

Edinburgh Castle

EUROPE

Eiffel Tower

Colosseum

Atlantic Ocean

Pacific Ocean

SOUTH AMERICA

Statue de Jesus

Did you know?
- Only 12 people have ever walked on the moon.
- It takes 45 minutes to put on a space suit.
- A spacecraft takes 3 days to travel from earth to the moon.

Did you know?
- The Eiffel tower is over 300 metres (984 feet) high.
- There are 1660 steps from the foot of the tower to the top.
- More than 2½ million rivets hold the tower together.
- In summer, the tower is 15 centimetres (6 inches) taller because of the warmer weather.

Look through the maps in this atlas to find the other places shown below.
▼

Arc de Triomphe

Golden Temple, Amritsar

terracotta soldier

Dome of the Rock

vi

Maps of each continent

How well do you know the flags of the world? Turn to the map of a continent and every flag will be shown beside its country. In addition all the statistics about the continent are listed. These include its highest mountain, longest river, biggest country and much more.

On every spread of a continent there is also a short activity which relates to the information shown on the map.

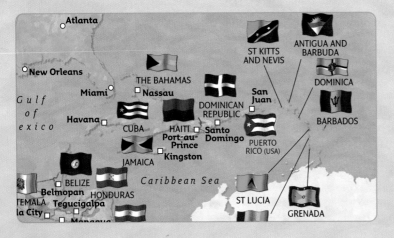

Atlanta

New Orleans

Miami

Havana

CUBA

Gulf of exico

THE BAHAMAS
Nassau

DOMINICAN REPUBLIC

HAITI
Port-au-Prince

Santo Domingo

Kingston

JAMAICA

San Juan

PUERTO RICO (USA)

ST KITTS AND NEVIS

ANTIGUA AND BARBUDA

DOMINICA

BARBADOS

BELIZE

Belmopan

HONDURAS

TEMALA
la City

Tegucigalpa

Caribbean Sea

ST LUCIA

GRENADA

Maps of regions and countries

Imagine you have just arrived in a new country. What will it be like? What do you want to do or see here?

The symbols placed on the countries can help you to decide. Look at the symbols in the neighbouring countries and plan a journey right across the region. There is so much to see and do.

Watch a Sumo wrestling match!
Take a train journey!

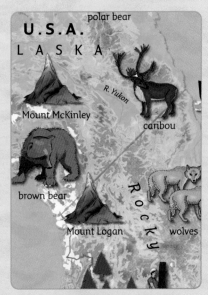

Go walking in the mountains!
See lots of animals!

Find out more from the facts placed around the maps.

It's a fact

The giant panda has lived in bamboo forests for several million years. Each year a panda can eat 5 tonnes of bamboo. There are only about 1600 left in the wild.

It's a fact

Ice hockey is one of Canada's most popular sports. It was first played in 1788 when some schoolboys tried to play the Irish game 'hurley' on ice. In Canada today there are over 500 000 players.

Try the activity found at the bottom of each map.

This will let you know just how much you have learnt from the map. All the answers are listed at the back of the atlas.

Try this!
China has many different animals. Look at the map and find

The big furry animal who loves to eat bamboo.

Many sports are played in Japan

Can you name 2 of these?

Try this!
Canada has many different animals and birds. Look at the map and find

4 types of bird
2 types of dog
3 furry wild animals

Where have you been?

You may like to see what other children think of the places they have visited or lived in. On pages 48–51 you can read some of the comments we have gathered from children. Have you been to the same places? What comment would you make about the places you have visited?

Kenya
We were in a big car and saw elephants and lions. I liked the lions but they had big teeth. It was very dusty and hot.
Katie

USA
I like Universal Studio because it has fantastic rides. I would give it a ten out of ten.
Sam

Index

You may know the name of a place you would like to visit but can't find the map it appears on. Turn to the index and find the name. The index will tell you which page in the atlas to turn to and where the place is on the map.

A

Aberdeen 24 C5
Abu Dhabi 35 D2
Abuja 18 C2
Accra 18 C2
Aconcagua 15 B4

Bamako 18 B3
Bandar Seri Begawan 40 C3
Bangkok 40 A4
Bangladesh 36 D4
Bangui 20 B6
Banjul 18 B3
Barbados 9 F2

World

The world is full of interesting places. Many countries have famous buildings like castles, churches and palaces and some of these are named on the map.

A r c t i c

N O R T H
A M E R I C A

Seattle Space Needle

Statue of Liberty

Kennedy Space Center

Mexican pyramid

Edinburgh Castle

EUROPE

Eiffel Tower

Colosseum

Atlantic

Ocean

A

Pacific

Ocean

S O U T H
A M E R I C A

Did you know?

- Only 12 people have ever walked on the moon.
- It takes 45 minutes to put on a space suit.
- A spacecraft takes 3 days to travel from earth to the moon.

Statue de Jesus

Did you know?

- The Eiffel tower is over 300 metres (984 feet) high.
- There are 1660 steps from the foot of the tower to the top.
- More than 2½ million rivets hold the tower together.
- In summer, the tower is 15 centimetres (6 inches) taller because of the warmer weather.

Look through the maps in this atlas to find the other places shown below.
▼

Arc de Triomphe

Golden Temple, Amritsar

terracotta soldier

Dome of the Rock

Interesting places

Kremlin

A S I A

Sphinx

Taj Mahal

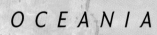

Great Wall of China

Pacific

Ocean

I C A

Indian

Ocean

Did you know?

- The Great Wall of China is the longest wall in the world.
- It winds up and down mountains and across fields and deserts.
- The wall is as tall as 2 double decker buses.

O C E A N I A

Sydney Opera House

Zulu house

Chilean chapel

Big Ben

Berber architecture

Angkor Wat

World

Animals and birds live all over the world. Each have their favourite places to live. This may depend on the climate and vegetation of the country in which they are found.

Arctic

Highland cattle

caribou

NORTH AMERICA

bobcat

puffin

EUROPE

bald eagle

gila monster

camel

Atlantic

Ocean

jaguar

pygmy hippopotamus

Pacific

Ocean

SOUTH AMERICA

alpaca

Did you know?

- Penguins are birds that cannot fly.
- They have waterproof feathers and are expert swimmers.
- The smallest penguin is called a Fairy Penguin.

Did you know?

- The giraffe is the tallest animal in the world. It can grow to more than 5 metres (16 feet) tall.
- A giraffe can live without water for longer than a camel. It can run faster than a horse.
- A giraffe can clean its ears with its very long tongue.

Look through the maps in this atlas to find the other animals and birds shown below.
▼

penguins

koala bear

poison arrow frog

spiny anteater

peacock

Animals and Birds

Ocean

lynx

brown bear

Siberian tiger

ASIA

Pacific

Ocean

giraffe

giant panda

gorilla

Indian

Ocean

RICA

OCEANIA

zebra

Did you know?

kangaroo

- A panda is a type of bear.
  It can climb trees.
- A baby panda is smaller
  than a mouse. When it is
  born, it cannot see.
- Pandas eat for up to
  16 hours every day.

kiwi

alligator

skunk

yak

snow goose

World

Different types of food are grown and eaten all over the world.
This map of the world shows where some of our favourite foods
are grown.

A r c t i c

NORTH
AMERICA

cranberries

apples

peanuts

hamburgers

cheese

EUROPE

pizza

dates

Atlantic

Ocean

bananas

A

Pacific

Ocean

oranges

SOUTH

AMERICA

Did you know?

- Apples can be all shades of red,
  green or yellow.
- One apple tree can produce 400
  apples every year.
- Apples can be as small as a cherry,
  or as large as a grapefruit.

grapes

Did you know?

- A coconut can float on the water.
- Coconuts are grown in more than
  90 countries of the world.
- You can drink coconut juice.
  It is the liquid found inside
  a coconut.

Look through the maps in this
atlas to find the other foods
shown below.
▼

tortilla

pumpkin pie

croissants

almonds

Food and Drink

potatoes

kebabs

wheat

ASIA

Pacific

Ocean

bowl of rice

tea

pineapples

Indian

Ocean

ICA

coconuts

Did you know?

seafood

OCEANIA

grapes

- Over half the people in the world eat rice every day.
- In China the word for rice is the same as the word for food.
- Rice is a type of grass. It is one of the oldest plants in the world.

kiwi fruit

spaghetti

olives

wheat

sardines

World

People play sport all over the world. Popular sports, like football, are played in almost every country. Different sports are shown on the map.

A r c t i c

N O R T H

A M E R I C A

snow boarding

cricket

EUROPE

ice hockey

rugby

American football

bull fighting

football

Atlantic

Ocean

Pacific

Ocean

football

S O U T H

A M E R I C A

surfing

motor racing

football

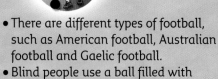
Did you know?

• There are different types of football, such as American football, Australian football and Gaelic football.
• Blind people use a ball filled with ball bearings, so that they can hear it.
• Bright orange footballs are used when it is snowy.

Did you know?

• Hockey can be played on ice, on a field or under the water.
• A hockey stick can be shaped like a J or an L.
• Hockey was played in Egypt thousands of years ago.

rug

polo

Look through the maps in this atlas to find the other sports and activities shown below.
▼

curling

baseball

skiing

yachting

Sports and Activities

e a n

chess

ASIA

karate

Pacific

Ocean

cricket

hockey

RICA

Indian

Ocean

Did you know?

- To surf you stand or lie on a board and float on the waves of the sea.
- Dolphins and whales like to surf the waves.
- The word surf can also mean to look at different pages of the World Wide Web on a computer.

Australian football

OCEANIA

tennis

cricket

surfing   rugby

sumo wrestling

lacrosse

scuba diving

gymnastics

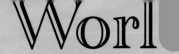
Worl

Seas and oceans cover two thirds of the earth's surface. The rest is land. The land is divided up into seven large masses of land known as continents.

Greenland

Arctic

Mount McKinley

Rocky Mountains

NORTH AMERICA

R. Missouri

R. Mississippi

Niagara Falls

Yosemite Falls

EUROP

Atlas Mountains

M

Sahar Deser

The map shows some of the largest features on each continent.

Caribbean Sea

Atlantic Ocean

Pacific

Ocean

Andes

Angel Falls

R. Amazon

SOUTH AMERICA

Andes

Did you know?

- Deserts cover a third of the world's surface.
- The Sahara is the world's largest desert.
- The highest sand dunes are found in Algeria.
- The highest temperatures in the world occur in the Sahara, however the nights can be very cold.

Did you know?

- The world's highest mountain range is Himalaya.
- Mount Everest is the highest peak at 8848 metres (29 029 feet).
- It was once known as Peak 15.
- Mount Everest was formed about 60 million years ago.
- Mount Everest was named after Sir George Everest the British surveyor-general of India.

Nam Dese

Iguazu Falls

Aconcagua

A global view of each continent is shown here. ▶

North America lies between the Atlantic and Pacific Oceans.

South America stretches from the Caribbean Sea towards the South Pole.

Europe is one of the smallest continents.

Natural Features

e a n

Ural Mountains

R. Ob'

R. Volga

S i b e r i a

Caucasus

Black Sea

El'brus

ASIA

Caspian Sea

Kunlun Shan

Gobi Desert

rranean Sea

Himalaya

Pacific Ocean

R. Nile

Arabian

R. Ganges

Mount Everest

Chang Jiang

Peninsula

Arabian Sea

Bay of Bengal

South China Sea

RICA

Indian Ocean

Borneo

R. Congo

Kilimanjaro

Puncak Jaya

New Guinea

Did you know?

ictoria Falls

- Angel Falls, in Venezuela, is the world's highest waterfall at 979 metres (3212 feet).
- Victoria Falls, on the Zambezi river between Zambia and Zimbabwe, is the largest. It is 1.7 kilometres (1 mile) wide and 128 metres (420 feet) high.
- Niagara Falls is the most powerful falls in North America.

Great Sandy Desert

Kalahari Desert

OCEANIA

Great Victoria Desert

Tugela Falls

Africa is almost equally balanced either side of the Equator.

Asia is the largest continent.

Oceania is made up of Australia and many small islands.

Antarctica encircles the South Pole.

World

Continents are divided up into many different countries. There are over 190 countries in the world. Lines are drawn on the map to show where two countries meet. These are known as international boundaries.

GREENLAND
(Denmark)

U.S.A.

CANADA

More detailed maps of Europe can be found on pages 22-29

UNITED STATES OF AMERICA

○ **Paris**
is the largest city in Europe

Azores
(Portugal)

TUNISIA

MOROCCO

ALGERIA   LIBY

MEXICO

THE BAHAMAS

WESTERN SAHARA

CUBA

Mexico City ○
is the largest city in North America

HAITI   DOMINICAN REP.

MAURITANIA

MALI   NIGER

GUATEMALA   BELIZE   JAMAICA

PUERTO RICO (USA)

CAPE VERDE   SENEGAL

CHA

EL SALVADOR   HONDURAS

NICARAGUA

THE GAMBIA

GUINEA-BISSAU   GUINEA

BURKINA

NIGERIA

This map also shows the largest city in each continent. ○

COSTA RICA

PANAMA

TRINIDAD & TOBAGO

VENEZUELA

GUYANA

SURINAME
FRENCH GUIANA

SIERRA LEONE

CÔTE D'IVOIRE

BENIN TOGO GHANA

CEN AFR REPU

LIBERIA

CAMEROON

EQUITORIAL GUINEA

COLOMBIA

Galapagos Is
(Ecuador)

ECUADOR

GABON

CONGO

P E R U

B R A Z I L

ANGO

Did you know?

BOLIVIA

Did you know?

PARAGUAY

○ **Sao Paulo**
is the largest city in South America

NAMI

When it is 12 noon in New York the time is
- 5 pm in London
- 3 am in Sydney
- 8 pm in Moscow
- Midnight in Bangkok
- 9 am in Los Angeles

C H I L E

A R G E N T I N A

URUGUAY

These countries have two capital cities.
- The Netherlands has The Hague and Amsterdam
- Malaysia has Kuala Lumpur and Putrajaya
- Bolivia has La Paz and Sucre
- South Africa has Pretoria and Cape Town
- Myanmar has Naypyidaw and Yangon

The flags of the eight largest countries in the world are shown below. Look through the rest of the atlas to find out more interesting facts about life in these countries.

Falkland Islands
(UK)

South Georgia
(UK)

▼

Russian Federation	Canada	China	United States of America

17 075 400 square kilometres	9 984 670 square kilometres	9 584 492 square kilometres	9 826 635 square kilometres
6 592 849 square miles	3 855 103 square miles	3 700593 square miles	3 794 085 square miles

Countries and Cities

RUSSIAN FEDERATION

KAZAKHSTAN

MONGOLIA

GEORGIA
ARMENIA AZERBAIJAN
UZBEKISTAN
KYRGYZSTAN
TURKMENISTAN
TAJIKISTAN

N. KOREA
JAPAN

TURKEY

CHINA

S. KOREA

Tokyo
is the largest city
in Asia

CYPRUS SYRIA
LEBANON
ISRAEL
JORDAN
IRAQ
IRAN
AFGHAN-
ISTAN

KUWAIT

PAKISTAN

NEPAL BHUTAN

Cairo
is the largest
city in Africa

SAUDI

BAHRAIN
QATAR
UNITED ARAB
EMIRATES

EGYPT

ARABIA OMAN

INDIA

BANGLA-
DESH

TAIWAN

MYANMAR
(BURMA)

LAOS

VIETNAM

Northern
Mariana Is.
(USA)

ERITREA YEMEN

THAILAND

SUDAN

PHILIPPINES

MARSHALL
ISLANDS

DJIBOUTI

CAMBODIA

ETHIOPIA

SOMALIA

SRI
LANKA

UGANDA

PALAU

FED. STATES OF
MICRONESIA

MOCRATIC
UBLIC
THE
NGO
KENYA
RWANDA
BURUNDI

MALDIVES

BRUNEI
MALAYSIA

NAURU

SINGAPORE

SEYCHELLES

TANZANIA

INDONESIA

PAPUA
NEW
GUINEA

SOLOMON
ISLANDS

COMOROS

EAST
TIMOR

VANUATU

AMBIA
MALAWI
MOZAMBIQUE

MAURITIUS

FIJI

ZIMBABWE

Did you know?

New
Caledonia
(France)

SWANA

MADAGASCAR

SWAZILAND

The time taken to fly between

AUSTRALIA

LESOTHO

• Los Angeles and Sydney is 14½ hours
• London and Tokyo is 12½ hours
• Paris and New York is 8½ hours
• Bangkok and Perth is 6¾ hours

P. OF
UTH
RICA

Sydney
is the largest city
in Oceania

NEW
ZEALAND

Îles Kerguélen
(France)

Brazil	Australia	India	Argentina
8 514 879 square kilometres	7 692 024 square kilometres	3 064 989 square kilometres	2 766 889 square kilometres
3 287 613 square miles	2 969 907 square miles	1 183 364 square miles	1 068 302 square miles

North America

North America is the largest continent in the western hemisphere. It is surrounded by great oceans: the Arctic to the north, the Pacific to the west and the Atlantic to the east. The countries of North America are a mixture of the large nations of Canada, USA and Mexico in the north and the tiny Caribbean island nations in the south. It is joined to South America by the narrow strip of land known as the isthmus of Panama.

People facts

- Population: 517 000 000
- Country with most people: United States of America 298 213 000
- City with most people: Mexico City 19 013 000

Geography facts

- Area: 24 680 331 square kilometres (9 529 129 square miles)
- Largest country: Canada 9 984 670 square kilometres (3 855 103 square miles)
- Longest river: Mississippi-Missouri 5969 kilometres (3709 miles)
- Highest mountain: Mount McKinley 6194 metres (20 321 feet)
- Largest lake: Lake Superior 82 100 square kilometres (31 698 square miles)
- Largest island: Greenland 2 175 600 square kilometres (840 004 square miles)

N
W — E
S

GREENLAND
(Denmark)

□ **Nuuk**

Baffin Bay

Baffin Island

Hudson Bay

CANADA

Arctic Ocean

Rocky

Bering Sea

ALASKA U.S.A.

▲ Mount McKinley

○ **Anchorage**

Atlantic Ocean

ANTIGUA AND BARBUDA

DOMINICA

BARBADOS

ST KITTS AND NEVIS

GRENADA

San Juan

PUERTO RICO (USA)

ST LUCIA

ST VINCENT AND THE GRENADINES

DOMINICAN REPUBLIC

Santo Domingo

HAITI
Port-au-Prince

Kingston

Bermuda (UK)

THE BAHAMAS

Nassau

CUBA

JAMAICA

Caribbean Sea

SOUTH AMERICA

Havana

BELIZE
Belmopan

HONDURAS

Tegucigalpa

NICARAGUA

Managua

Panama City

PANAMA

GUATEMALA
Guatemala City

San Salvador

EL SALVADOR

San José

COSTA RICA

Washington D.C.

Boston

New York

Montreal

Ottawa

Toronto

Detroit

Chicago

St Louis

Minneapolis

Lake Superior

R. Missouri

R. Mississippi

New Orleans

Atlanta

Miami

Dallas

Houston

Monterrey

UNITED STATES OF AMERICA

Denver

MEXICO

Guadalajara

Mexico City

Puebla

Phoenix

Los Angeles

San Francisco

Seattle

Pacific Ocean

Mountains

Gulf of Mexico

Did you know?

- The United States has over 250 000 rivers.

- There are over 10 000 glaciers on Baffin Island.

- The world's smallest volcano is in Puebla, Mexico.

- Belize's barrier reef at 285 kilometres (180 miles) is the longest in the western hemisphere.

- Some of the world's oldest rocks are found on the west coast of Greenland.

- 2 million caribou live in Canada.

Try this!

Unscramble these letters to find an island name.

Clue: It is the largest island in North America.

G L D E A N R E N

Answers at the back of the atlas.

3

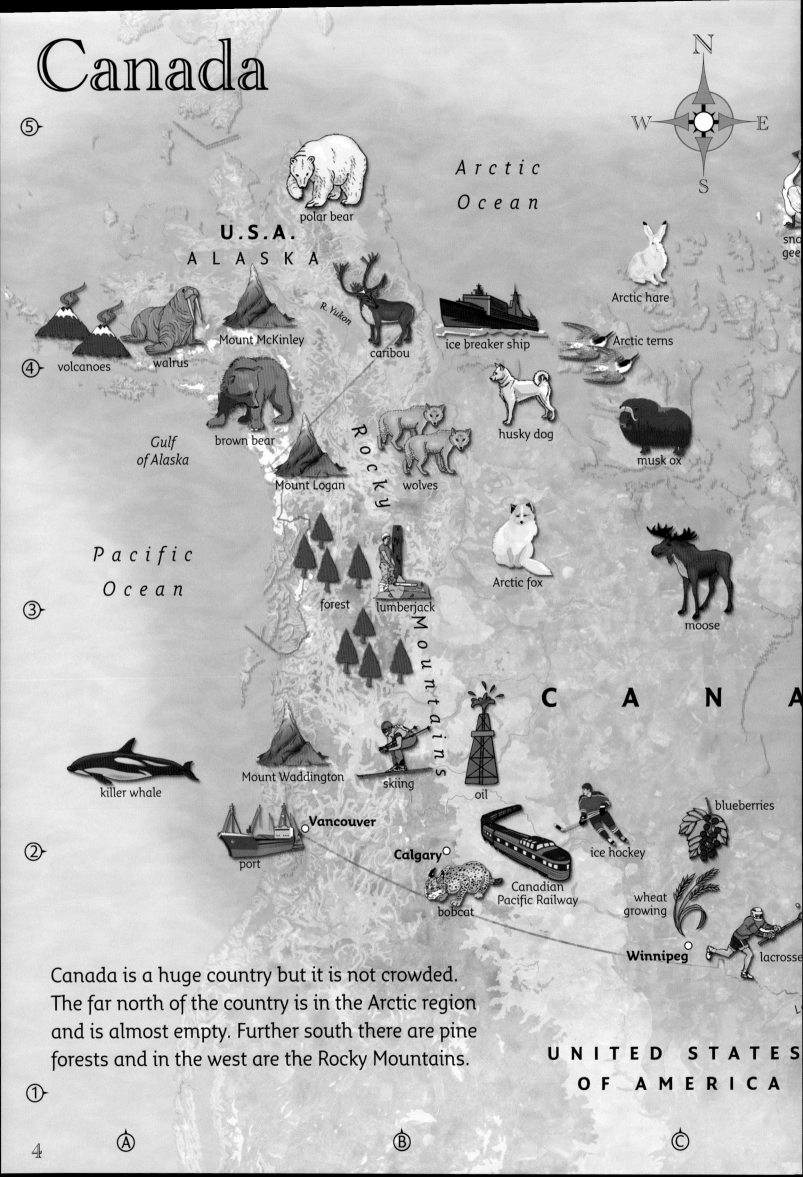

Canada

⑤

④

③

②

①

N
W E
S

Arctic Ocean

polar bear

U.S.A.

A L A S K A

R. Yukon

Mount McKinley

caribou

ice breaker ship

Arctic hare

sno
gee

Arctic terns

volcanoes

walrus

husky dog

musk ox

Gulf of Alaska

brown bear

Mount Logan

wolves

R o c k y

Arctic fox

moose

Pacific Ocean

forest

lumberjack

M o u n t a i n s

killer whale

Mount Waddington

skiing

oil

C A N A

Vancouver

port

Calgary

Canadian Pacific Railway

ice hockey

blueberries

wheat growing

bobcat

Winnipeg

lacrosse

Canada is a huge country but it is not crowded. The far north of the country is in the Arctic region and is almost empty. Further south there are pine forests and in the west are the Rocky Mountains.

U N I T E D   S T A T E S
O F   A M E R I C A

Ⓐ

Ⓑ

Ⓒ

4

polar bear

G r e e n l a n d
(Denmark)

seal

igloo

Inuit people

Baffin Island

it fishing

ptarmigan

Canadian goose

Nuuk
(Godthåb)

kayak

snowy owl

beluga whale

D   A

Hudson Bay

maple leaf

beaver

Newfoundland dog

*A t l a n t i c
O c e a n*

timber

maple syrup

lobster

R. St. Lawrence

curling

perior

apples

Quebec

apples

Ottawa church

Montreal

Lake Michigan

Lake Huron

Ottawa
cranberries

Toronto

Lake Ontario

Lake Erie

Niagara Falls

D

E

Did you know?

- Canada has the world's longest coastline – 202 000 kilometres (125 517 miles).
- The Arctic hare has huge feet which help it to run on top of the snow.
- Canadians consume more macaroni and cheese than any other nation on earth.

What am I?

- I grow on a tree at the end of a twig.
- I am the national emblem of Canada.
- I can be seen as a bright red symbol on my country's national flag.
- Canadians eat the syrup which is taken from the trunk of my tree.

What am I?

Try this!

Canada has many different animals and birds. Look at the map and find

4 types of bird
2 types of dog
3 furry wild animals

Answers at the back of the atlas.

It's a fact

Ice hockey is one of Canada's most popular sports. It was first played in 1788 when some schoolboys tried to play the Irish game 'hurley' on ice. In Canada today there are over 500 000 players.

5

United States of America

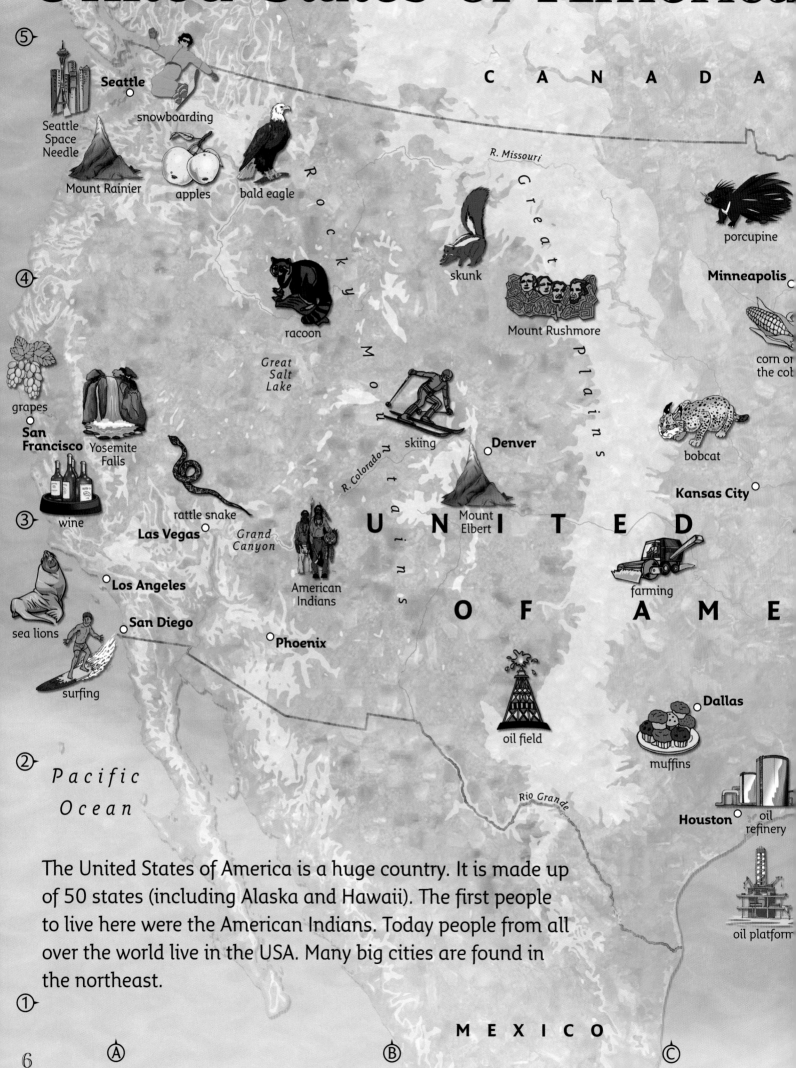

⑤

CANADA

Seattle

Seattle
Space
Needle

snowboarding

Mount Rainier

apples

bald eagle

R. Missouri

R
o
c
k
y

skunk

G
r
e
a
t

porcupine

Minneapolis

④

racoon

M
o
u
n
t
a
i
n
s

Mount Rushmore

P
l
a
i
n
s

corn on
the cob

Great
Salt
Lake

grapes

**San
Francisco**

Yosemite
Falls

wine

skiing

R. Colorado

Denver

bobcat

③

rattle snake

Las Vegas

Grand
Canyon

American
Indians

U N I T E D

Mount
Elbert

Kansas City

farming

sea lions

Los Angeles

San Diego

O F   A M E

surfing

Phoenix

oil field

Dallas

muffins

②

Pacific
Ocean

Rio Grande

Houston

oil
refinery

The United States of America is a huge country. It is made up
of 50 states (including Alaska and Hawaii). The first people
to live here were the American Indians. Today people from all
over the world live in the USA. Many big cities are found in
the northeast.

oil platform

①

M E X I C O

Ⓐ

Ⓑ

Ⓒ

A rattle snake is poisonous. Its tail makes a noise like a rattle. Sometimes rattle snakes can lose their tails, but a new one will grow. Every time the snake sheds its skin, a new segment is added to its tail. If it is very wet, the rattle may not make a noise.

blueberries

Lake Superior

Lake Michigan

Lake Huron

Lake Erie

Lake Ontario

Niagara Falls

purple finch

Boston

Statue of Liberty

skyscrapers

New York

Detroit

Chicago

lacrosse

Philadelphia

Liberty Bell

American football

baseball

Pittsburgh

Cincinnati

hamburgers

Capitol building

☐ **Washington D.C.**

St Louis

T A T E S

chipmunk

R. Mississippi

R I C A

Appalachian Mts

hot dog

Atlanta

peanuts

pumpkin pie

oranges

Kennedy Space Center

manatee

cruise ship

New Orleans

Miami

pink flamingo

THE BAHAMAS

alligator

Atlantic Ocean

Did you know?

- Between July and November there are often hurricanes in the south USA. These strong winds can destroy crops and buildings.

- The Great Lakes in the north of the country form some of the border between the USA and Canada.

- The world's first skyscrapers were built on Manhattan Island, in New York.

- The USA became an independent country on 4 July 1776. Today the fourth of July is a holiday called Independence Day.

What am I?

- I am something to eat.

- Americans eat about 7 billion of me each year.

- Many people eat me with tomato sauce or mustard.

- I can be called a frankfurter, wiener or weenie.

What am I?

Try this?

Many different types of food are grown and eaten in the USA.
Look at the map and find

4 types of fruit
3 types of snack
1 type of nut

Answers at the back of the atlas.

N
W   E
S

Gulf of Mexico

CUBA

D   E

Mexico and the Caribbean

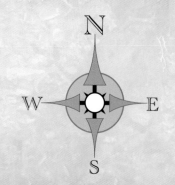

⑤ **Tijuana**

Ciudad Juárez

UNITED STATES

OF AMERICA

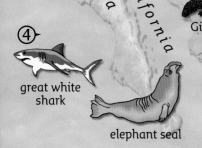
cactus

Gulf of California

Baja California

Sierra Madre

Río Grande

Gila monster

④
great white shark

elephant seal

Torreón

donkey

Tabasco sauce

Monterrey

Gulf of Mexico

tortilla

M E X I C O

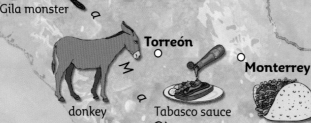

Did you know?

- The country name Panama means 'place of many fish'.

③
- It took over 30 years to build the Panama canal.

- Around 35 species of lobster live in the Caribbean Sea.

- In Tobago, goat racing is one of the most popular sports.

tacos ○

Guadalajara

○ **León**

football

Mexico City

Mexican hat

Toluca

Puebla

Mexican pyramid

Mexican temple

bull fighting

Yucatán

BELIZE

Belmopan □

coral re

GUATEMALA

Guatemala City □

H O N D

Tegucigal

San Salvador □

EL SALVADOR

sun bathing

red chilli

What am I?

- I like to live in hot, dry places.

- I can live without rain for a long time.

②
- I do not have leaves and I am often spiny.

- I can hold lots of water.

- Sometimes I am grown as a houseplant.

What am I?

turtle

Try this!

Many different species of fish and birds are found in this region.
Look at the map and find

6 types of fish and sea animals

① 2 types of bird

Pacific

Ocean

Answers at the back of the atlas.

The land between the USA and South America is known as Central America. Mexico is the largest country here. There is dry desert in northern Mexico and wet rainforest in southern Central America. The Caribbean is the area to the east, where there are hundreds of tropical islands.

Bermuda

Atlantic Ocean

cruise ship

□ **Nassau**

THE BAHAMAS

Turks and Caicos Islands

Havana □

CUBA

cigars

Monarch butterfly

sugar cane

mangoes

reggae singer

limes

DOMINICAN REPUBLIC

Santo Domingo □

parrot

San Juan □

cruise ship

ST KITTS AND NEVIS

Anguilla

HAITI

Port-au-Prince □

PUERTO RICO

ANTIGUA AND BARBUDA

Montserrat

Guadeloupe

Cayman Is

scuba diving

butterflies

JAMAICA

Rum

Kingston □

rum

gourds

bananas

radio telescope

sea horse

volcano

DOMINICA

Martinique

ST LUCIA

pineapples

C a r i b b e a n   S e a

ST VINCENT AND THE GRENADINES

BARBADOS

GRENADA

AS

bananas

ICARAGUA

Managua

Lake Nicaragua

toucan

tropical fish

monk seal

Aruba

oil platform

yachting

TRINIDAD & TOBAGO

cricket

COSTA RICA

□ **San José**

Panama Canal

VENEZUELA

Panama City □

PANAMA

coconuts

coffee

monkey

It's a fact

Sea horses are a species of fish. They live in warm tropical waters. They eat slowly, sucking up food through their long noses. Sea horses can move their eyes all around, without moving their bodies. They wrap their long, curly tails around seaweed to stay in one place.

COLOMBIA

Ⓓ   Ⓔ   Ⓕ

South America

⑦ South America stretches farther south from the equator than all the other continents. The longest mountain range in the world, the Andes, runs the full length of the continent. The Amazon rainforest is the largest in the world. Colourful birds and butterflies, giant snakes, jaguars, monkeys and pumas can all be found in this lush forest. People speak Portuguese in Brazil, but Spanish in other countries.

⑥

⑤

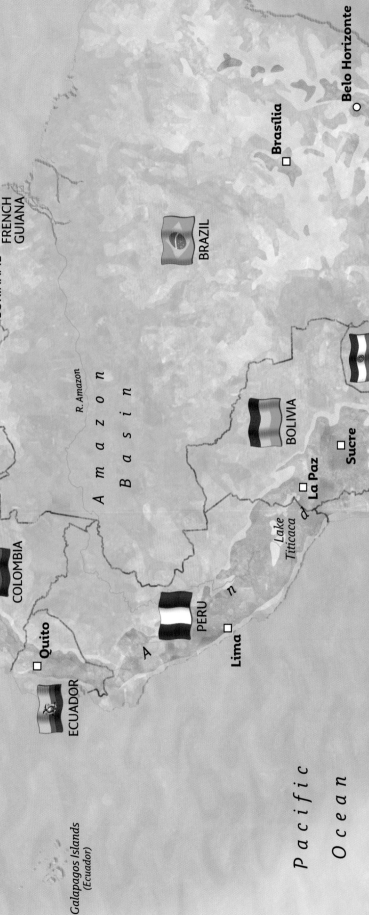

N
W · E
S

Atlantic Ocean

Pacific Ocean

TRINIDAD & TOBAGO
Port of Spain

Caracas
VENEZUELA

Cayenne
FRENCH GUIANA

Paramaribo
SURINAME

Georgetown
GUYANA

Bogotá
COLOMBIA

Quito
ECUADOR

Galapagos Islands
(Ecuador)

Lima
PERU

R. Amazon

Amazon Basin

A n d

Lake Titicaca

La Paz
BOLIVIA

Sucre

BRAZIL

Brasília

Belo Horizonte

São Paulo

Rio de Janeiro

Did you know?

- La Paz is the world's highest capital city.

- Columbia was named after Christopher Columbus.

- More than 2000 different species of butterflies are found in the rainforests of South America.

- Alpacas live in the mountains of Peru, Bolivia and Chile. They come in over 22 colours and do not like being touched.

- Ecuador is the world's leading exporter of bananas.

Asunción

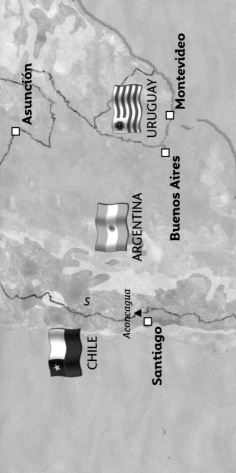

URUGUAY

Montevideo

Buenos Aires

ARGENTINA

Aconcagua

S

Santiago

CHILE

Falkland
Islands
(UK)

Tierra del
Fuego

South Georgia
(UK)

ANTARCTICA

Southern Ocean

People facts

- Population: 375 000 000

- Country with most people: Brazil 186 405 000

③ City with most people: São Paulo 18 333 000

Geography facts

- Area: 17 815 420 square kilometres (6 878 572 square miles)

- Largest country: Brazil 8 514 879 square kilometres (3 287 613 square miles)

- Longest river: Amazon 6516 kilometres (4049 miles)

② Highest mountain: Aconcagua 6959 metres (22 834 feet)

- Largest lake: Lake Titicaca 8340 square kilometres (3220 square miles)

- Largest island: Tierra del Fuego 47 000 square kilometres (18 147 square miles)

Try this!

Find 2 countries beginning with the letter C.

Find 2 capital cities beginning with the letter B.

Answers at the back of the atlas.

① ② ③ ④

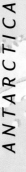

Ⓐ Ⓑ Ⓒ Ⓓ

South America North

Most people in this area live on the low land near the coast.
Ecuador is the Spanish word for equator. The equator is an
imaginary line around the middle of the earth. Many unique
species of animal live in the area. Potatoes, peppers and
beans have been grown here for thousands of years.

④

Caribbean
Sea

Barranquilla
Cartagena

Maracaibo

Caracas

Port of Spain

TRINIDAD
& TOBAGO

Barquisimeto

Valencia

oil refineries

oil
wells

PANAMA

R. Orinoco

VENEZUELA

GUYAN

Bucaramanga

iguana

jaguar

Medellín

puma

Angel
Falls

poison
arrow
frog

Bogotá

Guiana

③

coffee

emeralds

Cali

COLOMBIA

R. Negro

H

slot

Quito

Mount
Cotopaxi

coffee

butterflies

Manau

ECUADOR

manta ray

tapir

football

Guayaquil

capybara

Amazon

Basin

②

condor

panpipes

monkeys

anaconda

R. Madeira

B

Pacific
Ocean

llama

deforestation

①

Andes

PERU

rubber

BOLIVIA

Lima

Ⓐ

coffee

Ⓑ

Ⓒ

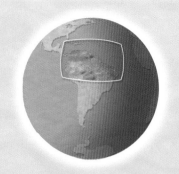

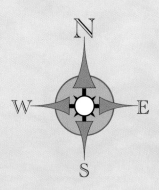

N
W · E
S

It's a fact

Andean panpipes are musical instruments made from pipes strapped together. The pipes are made from a reed called 'songo'. Songo grows on the banks of Lake Titicaca. Andean panpipes are also called zampoñas.

Did you know?

- The River Amazon carries more water than the rivers Nile, Chang Jiang and Mississippi combined.

- The Amazon is the largest rainforest in the world. About half of the world's plants, animals and insects are found there.

- The world's highest railway station, La Galera, is in Peru.

What am I?

- I live in the mountains and can reach more than 50 years of age.

- I can glide through the air for very long distances.

- Sometimes I eat so much that I can't get off the ground to fly.

- I am one of the world's largest vultures.

What am I?

Try this!

Look at the map and find

2 precious stones
1 deadly snake

Answers at the back of the atlas.

eorgetown

Paramaribo

rocket launch

Cayenne

SURINAME   FRENCH GUIANA

h l a n d s

cayenne peppers

R. Amazon

Belém

A t l a n t i c
O c e a n

Fortaleza

toucan

armadillo

sugar cane

Natal

R   A   Z   I   L

surfing

R. São Francisco

Recife

porcupines

R. Tocantins

Maceió

parrot

B r a z i l i a n
H i g h l a n d s

D   diamonds

E

Salvador

F

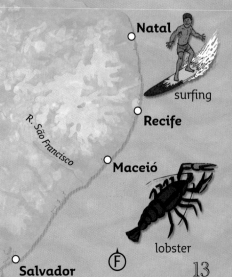

lobster

13

South America South

Running down the west coast of this area is the driest place on earth, the Atacama Desert. The southern tip of South America is very cold and there are icebergs in the sea. Many people in Paraguay are descended from the Indians who lived in South America before people from Europe arrived.

N
W — E
S

Planalto do
Mato Grosso

Brazilian
Highlands

P E R U

B O L I V I A

B R A Z I L

PARAGUAY

Brasília

Goiânia

Campinas
São Paulo
Santos
Curitiba

Belo Horizonte

Statue de Jesus
Rio de Janeiro

beaches

carnivals

oranges

coffee growing

footballer

football
Asunción

Iguaçu Falls

Porto Alegre

R. Paraná

R. Paraguay

Gran
Chaco

Santa Cruz

Sucre

La Paz
skiing

Lake
Titicaca

alpaca

potatoes

Atacama   Desert

man in
poncho

Chilean
stag beetle

anteater

chinchilla

pelican

sheep

Argentinian
church

R. Paraná

R. Salado

A
N

Did you know?

- Chile is 10 times longer than it is wide.
- The sea around Cape Horn, south of Chile, is very rough. Many ships have

14

wine
Aconcagua
Córdoba
Rosario
URUGUAY
oil tanker
Santiago
Mendoza
wine
polo
Buenos Aires
Montevideo
Rio de la Plata
grapes
vineyards
motor racing
fishing boats
Chilean chapel
gaucho
sardines
tango dancers
R. Negro
Pampas
CHILE
ARGENTINA
Pacific Ocean
puma
Patagonia
southern whale
glaciers
elephant seals
albatross
Atlantic Ocean
Falkland Islands (UK)
Tierra del Fuego
killer whale
penguins
Cape Horn
South Georgia (UK)
mackerel
3
2
1
A
B
C
D

It's a fact

Anteaters eat ants and termites. They have a long, sticky tongue and no teeth. Their front claws are strong and sharp. The babies ride on their mother's back.

Spanish.

- Millions of sheep and cattle are farmed on the flat grassy plains known as the pampas. They are looked after by Gauchos, or cowboys.
- Almost all of Paraguay's electricity comes from hydroelectric power.
- Uruguay has won several Olympic medals for football.

What am I?

- I live in the sea.
- I am black and white and have a large fin.
- I am very sociable and have a good memory.
- I am noisy. I make lots of clicks and whistles.
- I have been around for millions of years.
- I can be called Orca.

What am I?

Try this!

Look at the map and find

2 types of fish

Many sports are played in South America

Can you name 3 of these?

Answers at the back of the atlas.

Africa

Africa is the second largest continent. It is 3 times the area of Europe. From the Mediterranean Sea in the north, Africa stretches approximately 8000 kilometres (4971 miles) to its most southerly point, Cape Agulhas. Most of northern Africa lies in and around the Sahara desert, while large areas of central Africa are covered in dense tropical rainforest.

People facts

- Population: 909 000 000
- Country with most people: Nigeria 131 530 000
- City with most people: Cairo 11 146 000

Geography facts

- Area: 30 343 578 square kilometres (11 715 721 square miles)
- Largest country: Sudan 2 505 813 square kilometres (967 500 square miles)
- Longest river: Nile 6695 kilometres (4160 miles)
- Highest mountain: Kilimanjaro 5892 metres (19 331 feet)
- Largest lake: Lake Victoria 68 800 square kilometres (26 563 square miles)
- Largest island: Madagascar 587 040 square kilometres (226 657 square miles)

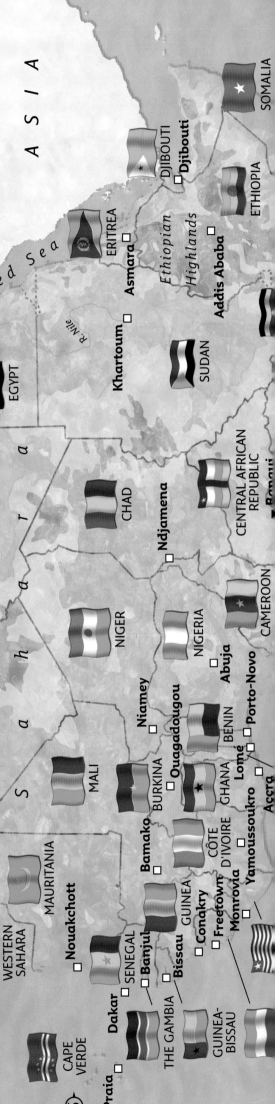

EUROPE

ASIA

Azores (Portugal)

Madeira (Portugal)

Canary Is (Spain)

Mediterranean Sea

Red Sea

R. Nile

Atlas Mountains

Sahara

Ethiopian Highlands

MOROCCO — Rabat

WESTERN SAHARA — Laayoune

ALGERIA — Algiers

TUNISIA — Tunis

LIBYA — Tripoli

EGYPT — Cairo

MAURITANIA — Nouakchott

MALI — Bamako

NIGER — Niamey

CHAD — Ndjamena

SUDAN — Khartoum

ERITREA — Asmara

DJIBOUTI — Djibouti

ETHIOPIA — Addis Ababa

SOMALIA

CAPE VERDE — Praia

SENEGAL — Dakar

THE GAMBIA — Banjul

GUINEA-BISSAU — Bissau

GUINEA — Conakry

SIERRA LEONE — Freetown

LIBERIA — Monrovia

CÔTE D'IVOIRE — Yamoussoukro

BURKINA — Ouagadougou

GHANA — Accra

TOGO — Lomé

BENIN — Porto-Novo

NIGERIA — Abuja

CAMEROON

CENTRAL AFRICAN REPUBLIC — Bangui

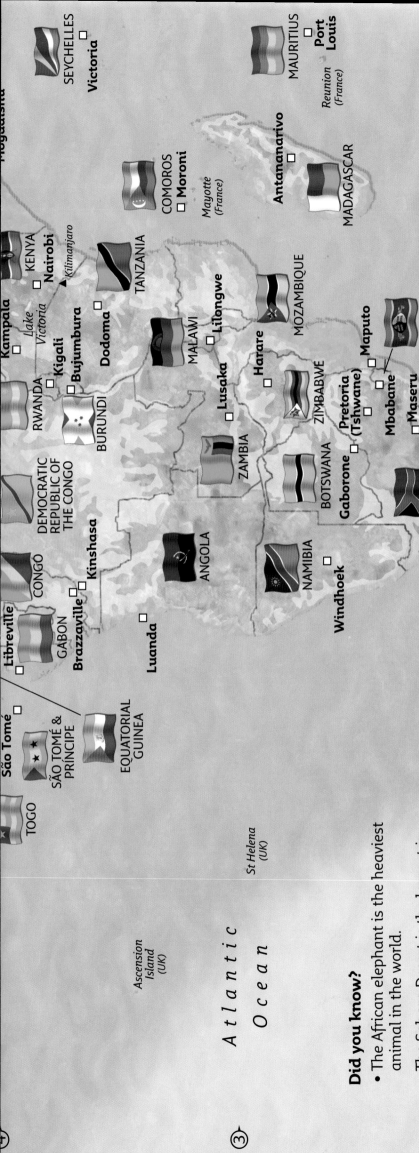

SEYCHELLES
Victoria

MAURITIUS
Port Louis

Reunion
(France)

COMOROS
Moroni

Mayotte
(France)

Antananarivo

MADAGASCAR

Indian Ocean

KENYA
Nairobi
▲ *Kilimanjaro*

Kampala

Lake Victoria

TANZANIA

RWANDA
Kigali
Bujumbura
BURUNDI
Dodoma

MALAWI
Lilongwe

Lusaka
ZAMBIA

Harare

MOZAMBIQUE
ZIMBABWE

Maputo
SWAZILAND
Mbabane

Pretoria (Tshwane)
Maseru
LESOTHO

BOTSWANA
Gaborone

REPUBLIC OF SOUTH AFRICA
Cape Agulhas

NAMIBIA
Windhoek

Cape Town

DEMOCRATIC REPUBLIC OF THE CONGO
Kinshasa

CONGO
GABON
Libreville
Brazzaville

ANGOLA
Luanda

St Helena
(UK)

São Tomé
SÃO TOMÉ & PRÍNCIPE

EQUATORIAL GUINEA

TOGO

Ascension Island
(UK)

Atlantic Ocean

Did you know?

- The African elephant is the heaviest animal in the world.

- The Sahara Desert is the largest in the world and nearly as big as the whole of Europe.

- Mount Kenya is on the equator, but its peak is always covered in snow.

- About 400 languages are spoken in Nigeria.

- The Goliath beetle found near the equator in Africa is one of the largest insects in the world.

- In the rainforests of central Africa, it rains almost every day.

- The sea around the Cape of Good Hope is rough and dangerous. Gale force winds blow there most of the time.

Try this!

Unscramble these letters to find the country.
Clue: It is surrounded by sea.

CARDAMSAGA

Answers at the back of the atlas.

Ⓐ   Ⓑ   Ⓒ   Ⓓ

① ② ③ ④

17

Northern Africa

Did you know?

- There are over 500 tribes in Sudan. The tribes speak more than 100 different languages.

- Although there are many different languages, most people in northern Africa can speak Arabic.

- In Nigeria, twins are always called the same names. The first twin is called Taiwo. The second twin is called Kehinde.

- In Egypt, many people live on the banks of the River Nile, where they can grow food.

- Lake Chad is very shallow and is shrinking fast.

What am I?

- I am used for transport, milk, meat and wool.

- I can survive without water for about 2 weeks and without food for around a month.

- My thick coat reflects sunshine and my long eyelashes protect my eyes from sand.

- I can have one or two humps.

What am I?

Answers at the back of the atlas.

PORTUGAL
SPAIN

Mediter

Algiers

spices

citrus fruit

grapes

Rabat
Casablanca

MOROCCO

Madeira (Portugal)

Atlas Mts

Berber architecture

carpets

oasis

Canary Is (Spain)

Laayoune

WESTERN SAHARA

ALGERIA

S   a

date palm

sand dune

dates

cactus

MAURITANIA

baboon

camel

MALI

CAPE VERDE

Nouakchott

R. Sénégal

R. Niger

Praia

③

Dakar

SENEGAL

Banjul

THE GAMBIA

S   a   h   e   l

N I

beach resort

Bissau

GUINEA-BISSAU

pygmy hippopotamus

Bamako

groundnuts

Niamey

BURKINA

Ouagadougou

hoopoe

Conakry

GUINEA

Freetown

GHANA

BENIN

N I G E

SIERRA LEONE

bananas

CÔTE D'IVOIRE

cocoa

Abuja

Monrovia

Yamoussoukro

TOGO

Lake Volta

Lomé

football

LIBERIA

Accra

Porto-Novo

Lagos

coconuts

Gulf of Guinea

Mt Camero

Malabo

EQUATORIAL GUINEA

oil

São Tomé

Atlantic Ocean

SÃO TOMÉ AND PRÍNCIPE

Librevi

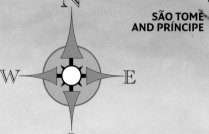

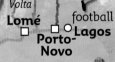

N

W — E

S

① ② ③ ④

peninsula, north of the Red Sea. It is separated narrowly from Europe by the Strait of Gibraltar. Much of northern Africa is dry desert: the Sahara Desert and the Sahel region.

ean
nis
ach resort
ISIA

Sea

□ **Tripoli**

fishing

cruise ship

ISRAEL

JORDAN

olives

Cairo □

sphinx

L I B Y A

a

oil

a

r

a

Suez Canal

scorpion

desert safari

E G Y P T

Lake Nasser

R. Nile

R e d

Try this?

Many different animals and birds are found in this region.
Look at the map and find

3 types of animal with furry or woolly coats
2 types of animal with hard shells
3 types of bird

Answers at the back of the atlas.

S A U D I
A R A B I A

gerbil

gourds

dhow

S

Bedouin tent

crocodile

ERITREA

Asmara □

Y E M E N

R

Khartoum □

e

a

Gulf of Aden

C H A D

tortoise

Lake Chad

□ **Ndjamena**

S U D A N

R. White Nile

R. Blue Nile

Lake Tana

Ras Dejen

DJIBOUTI
□ **Djibouti**

hoopoe

A

R. Benue

E t h i o p i a n

Addis Ababa □

bee eater bird

C E N T R A L
A F R I C A N
R E P U B L I C

secretary bird

H i g h l a n d s

E T H I O P I A

Lake Turkana

S
O
M
A
L
I
A

□ **Yaoundé**

Bangui □

hornbill bird

Webi Shabeelle

□ **Mogadishu**

AMEROON

gorilla

UGANDA

K E N Y A

I n d i a n
O c e a n

GABON

DEMOCRATIC

It's a fact

CONGO

REPUBLIC

OF THE CONGO

Dhows are traditional wooden boats. They have been used along the north and east coasts of Africa for thousands of years. Their triangular sails are called lateens. Dhows are used to transport people, animals, fish and other goods.

ANGOLA

Ⓓ

Ⓔ **TANZANIA**

Ⓕ

Southern Africa

At the centre of southern Africa is the huge rainforest of the River Congo and the Congo Basin. The Great Rift Valley is surrounded by some of the highest mountains in Africa. In the southwest are the Kalahari and Namib deserts.

N E S W

ERITREA

DJIBOUTI

SOMALIA

Mogadishu

ETHIOPIA

Ethiopian Highlands

SUDAN

secretary bird

KENYA

Lake Turkana

elephants

coffee beans

lion

Kilimanjaro

beaches

cloves
Dar es Salaam

Indian Ocean

Nairobi

Lake Victoria

UGANDA

Kampala

Dodoma

TANZANIA

leopard

MALA

Moroni
COMOROS

MAYOTTE

Lake Nyasa

chameleon

Great Rift Valley

gorilla

Kigali
RWANDA

Bujumbura
BURUNDI

Lake Tanganyika

cheetah
Lubumbashi

Lilongwe

CENTRAL AFRICAN REPUBLIC

hornbill bird

DEMOCRATIC

R. Congo

REPUBLIC

OF

THE

CONGO

Bangui

crocodiles

Congo Basin

elephants

deforestation

NIGERIA

CAMEROON

Yaoundé

chimpanzee

Brazzaville

Kinshasa

ANGOLA

Malabo

EQUATORIAL GUINEA

Libreville
GABON

São Tomé

SÃO TOMÉ AND PRÍNCIPE

C O N G O

flying fish

Luanda

ANGOLA

Bie Plateau

oil rig

20

⑦

⑥

⑤

MADAGASCAR

□ Antananarivo

crocodiles

lemur

Mozambique Channel

aardvark

port

ZAMBIA

□ Lusaka

R. Zambezi

□ Harare

ZIMBABWE

Victoria Falls

rhinoceros

R. Linpopo

MOZAMBIQUE

□ **Maputo**

□ **Mbabane**
SWAZILAND

Zulu warrior

Zulu house

○ **Durban**

sharks

BOTSWANA

□ **Gaborone**

Kalahari Desert

meerkat

oryx

□ **Pretoria (Tshwane)**

○ Johannesburg

gold mines

□ **Maseru**
LESOTHO

Drakensberg

R. Orange

NAMIBIA

rhinoceros

□ **Windhoek**

rugby

sand dunes

Namib Desert

ostrich

oranges

grapes

**REPUBLIC OF
SOUTH AFRICA**

○ **Port Elizabeth**

cricket

□ **Cape Town**
*Cape of
Good Hope*

penguins

A t l a n t i c
O c e a n

sardines

What am I?

- I am found on the coast and in deserts.
- I can be made from worn down stone and shell.
- I move in the wind and get very hot in the sun.
- I can be different shapes: ridges, crescents and crests like waves.
- I can fall downhill in an avalanche, like snow.
- I am made from sand.

What am I?

Try this?

There are lots of different fruits and plants in this region.
Look at the map and find

2 types of fruit
1 type of spice.

Answers at the back of the atlas.

Ⓓ

Ⓒ

It's a fact

Gorillas are the largest type of monkey in the world. They live on the ground in the forests of Africa. Gorillas are a close relative to humans. They eat fruits, leaves and insects. Gorillas are in danger of becoming extinct.

Ⓑ

Did you know?

- Madagascar is the only place in the world where lemurs live.
- A lemur is a type of monkey with a long tail.
- Nelson Mandela became the first black president of South Africa in 1994.
- European languages such as French, Portuguese and English are widely spoken in southern Africa.
- Diamonds and gold are mined in southern Africa.

Ⓐ

21

Europe

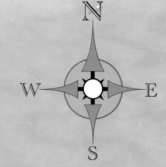

The land area of Europe covers just over 2% of the world. It is the second smallest continent and extends far north into the Arctic Ocean and south to the Mediterranean Sea. In the north the winters are long and cold. In the south the weather is much warmer. Europe has over 40 countries and a wide variety of cultures, languages and religions.

People facts
- Population: 586 000 000 (excluding Russian Federation)
- Country with most people: Germany 82 689 000
- City with most people: Paris 9 854 000

Geography facts
- Area: 9 908 599 square kilometres (3 825 731 square miles)
- Largest country: Ukraine 603 700 square kilometres (233 090 square miles) (excluding Russian Federation)
- Longest river: Volga 3688 kilometres (2291 miles)
- Highest mountain: El'brus 5642 metres (18 510 feet)
- Largest lake: Caspian Sea 371 000 square kilometres (143 243 square miles)
- Largest island: Great Britain 218 476 square kilometres (84 354 square miles)

Try this!

How many flags are black, red and yellow?

Which flag has 5 blue stripes?

Which country uses this flag?

Answers at the back of the atlas.

ICELAND
Reykjavík

Faroe Islands (Denmark)

UNITED KINGDOM

Dublin

Great Britain

IRELAND

NETHERLAN
Amsterda
The
Hague
London

Brusse

BELGIUM

Atlantic Ocean

Paris

LUXEMBOU
Be

FRANCE

SWITZERLA

ANDORRA

MONACO

PORTUGAL

Madrid

Barcelona

Lisbon

SPAIN

Gibraltar (UK)

A F R I C A

22

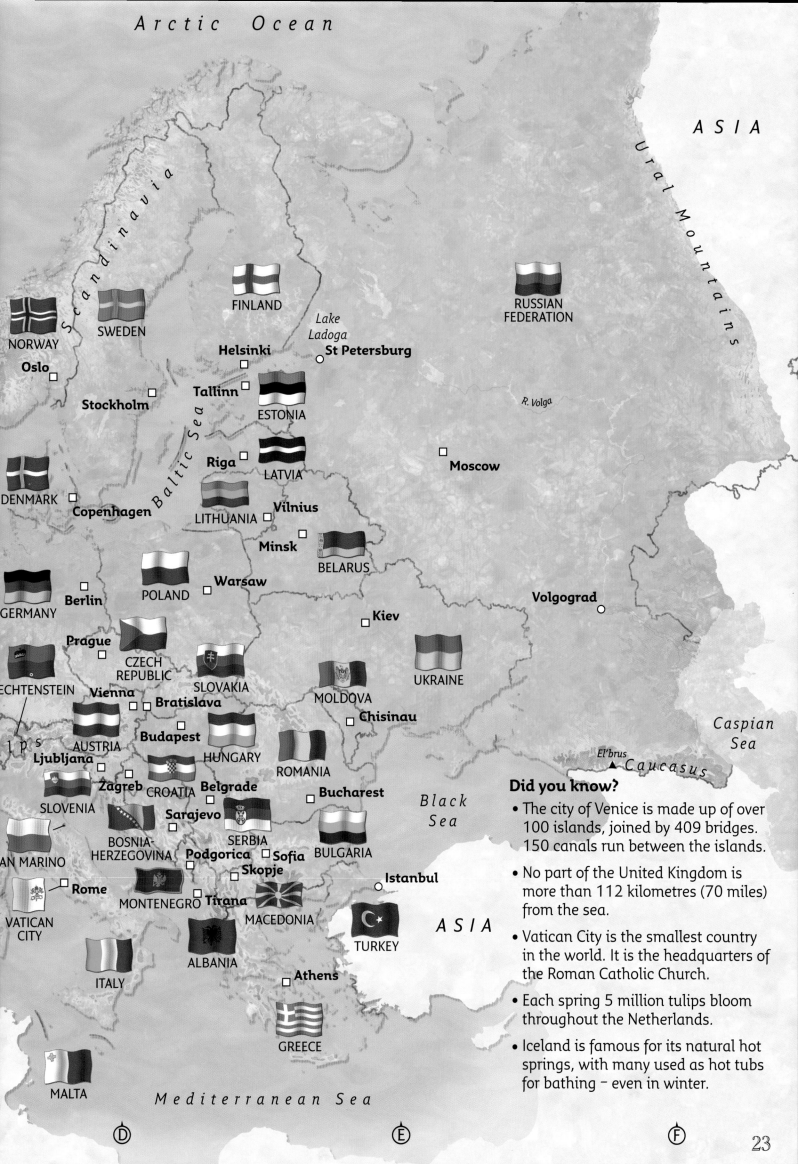

Arctic Ocean

ASIA

Ural Mountains

Scandinavia

NORWAY

Oslo

SWEDEN

Stockholm

FINLAND

Helsinki

Lake Ladoga

St Petersburg

RUSSIAN FEDERATION

R. Volga

Tallinn

ESTONIA

Baltic Sea

Riga

LATVIA

Moscow

DENMARK

Copenhagen

Vilnius

LITHUANIA

Minsk

BELARUS

Volgograd

GERMANY

Berlin

POLAND

Warsaw

Kiev

Prague

CZECH REPUBLIC

SLOVAKIA

UKRAINE

LIECHTENSTEIN

Vienna

Bratislava

MOLDOVA

Caspian Sea

l p s

AUSTRIA

Budapest

Chisinau

Ljubljana

HUNGARY

El'brus

Caucasus

Zagreb

CROATIA

Belgrade

ROMANIA

SLOVENIA

Bucharest

Black Sea

Sarajevo

SAN MARINO

BOSNIA-HERZEGOVINA

Podgorica

SERBIA

Sofia

BULGARIA

Skopje

Rome

MONTENEGRO

Tirana

Istanbul

VATICAN CITY

MACEDONIA

TURKEY

ASIA

ALBANIA

ITALY

Athens

GREECE

MALTA

Mediterranean Sea

Did you know?

- The city of Venice is made up of over 100 islands, joined by 409 bridges. 150 canals run between the islands.

- No part of the United Kingdom is more than 112 kilometres (70 miles) from the sea.

- Vatican City is the smallest country in the world. It is the headquarters of the Roman Catholic Church.

- Each spring 5 million tulips bloom throughout the Netherlands.

- Iceland is famous for its natural hot springs, with many used as hot tubs for bathing – even in winter.

D

E

F

23

United Kingdom and Ireland

The United Kingdom is made up of 4 nations: England, Wales, Scotland and Northern Ireland. Its capital and largest city is London. Great Britain is the largest island in Europe and is separated from mainland Europe by only 35 kilometres (21 miles) at the Strait of Dover. Ireland, whose capital is Dublin, is a separate country from Northern Ireland.

Try this!

Many different sports are popular in the United Kingdom. Look at the map and find

3 sports played with a ball
1 sport that takes place on water
2 sports that need ice or snow

Answers at the back of the atlas.

Did you know?

- More than 6000 islands make up the United Kingdom and Ireland.
- Some areas of Ireland have more wet days than dry days.
- The city of Edinburgh is built on an extinct volcano.
- More than 300 different languages are spoken in London.
- The Welsh language is spoken and written in Wales.
- Many tourists come to these islands to visit the castles, churches and ancient buildings.
- Football, rugby and cricket are popular sports.

What am I?

- I am green. Mostly I have white flowers.
- I usually have 3 leaves.
- Ancient people thought I was magical.
- I am strongly associated with Ireland.

What am I?

Answers at the back of the atlas.

Shetland Islands

Orkney Islands

Atlantic Ocean

Outer Hebrides

Lewis

The Minch

Skye

golden eagle

Inner Hebrides

Highland cattle

Moray Firth

Inverness

Loch Ness

skiing

oil rig

Aberdeen

fishing boat

Grampian Mts

Ben Nevis

Fort William

S C O T L A N D

Highland piper

Dundee

curling

Jura

Islay

Glasgow

Edinburgh

Firth of Forth

Edinburgh Castle

North

N W E S

North Sea

fishing boat

U N I T E D

Newcastle
upon Tyne

Middlesbrough

R. Tyne

R. Tees

cathedral

K I N G D O M

The Pennines

York

Leeds
Bradford

rose

Sheffield

Manchester

Nottingham
Derby

R. Trent

cricket

Stoke-on-Trent

E N G L A N D

Leicester

The Wash

Norwich

Norfolk
Broads

Ipswich

port

Southend-on-Sea

Big
Ben

Tower
Bridge

London

Cambridge

London bus

R. Thames

Reading

football

Oxford

Wolverhampton

Birmingham

R. Severn

rugby

Bristol

Stonehenge

Brighton

Southampton
Portsmouth

Isle of
Wight

yachting

Bournemouth

Torquay

English Channel

Isle
of Man

Manx cat

Blackpool

Preston

Liverpool

Anglesey

Irish Sea

sheep

Cambrian
Mountains

W A L E S

daffodil

Cardiff

Bristol Channel

Swansea

Cardigan
Bay

St George's Channel

Celtic Sea

windsurfing

Plymouth

Land's End

Isles of
Scilly

thistle

Solway Firth

North Channel

U

Londonderry

N O R T H E R N

Lough
Neagh

I R E L A N D

Belfast

Dundalk Bay

Dundalk

harp

Dublin courthouse

Dublin

port

I R E L A N D

shamrock

Waterford

crystal glass

Cork

Irish
dancers

Guinness

Limerick

Galway

Galway Bay

potatoes

Donegal Bay

dairy farming

R. Shannon

yachting

It's a fact

Red buses have been used in London
since the 1950s. They replaced trams
and trolley buses. They can be single
or double decked. Open-topped buses
are popular with tourists. The London
bus network is one of the largest in the
world. Every weekday 6 million passengers
are carried over 700 different routes.

FRANCE

A B C D

1 2 3 4

25

Northern Europe

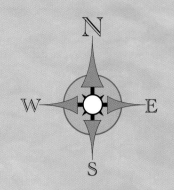
glaciers

□ **Reykjavik**

ICELAND

Northern Europe has a rugged landscape and many of its countries are almost completely surrounded by sea. In the far north winters can be extremely cold and the seas may freeze for several months. Most people live in the south of this region where the climate is milder.

Faroe Is (Denmark)

Did you know?

- The Baltic Sea borders on 9 countries. Parts of it can be frozen for 6 months of the year.
- Brittany is a region in northwest France. The people there speak Breton.
- Puppets are popular in the Czech Republic. They are used to entertain people and tell stories.
- German is spoken in Austria, Switzerland and Germany.

What am I?

- I have large round eyes, a sharp beak and claws.
- I fly about at night and I sleep during the day.
- I hunt small animals, insects and fish.
- I build nests in trees, barns and sometimes underground.

What am I?

Try this!

Many different types of food are grown or manufactured in this region. Look at the map and find

    1 type of cheese
    3 types of farm animal
    1 type of pastry

Answers at the back of the atlas.

salmon

fishing boats

oil rigs

Norwegian church

DEN

Highland piper

Edinburgh Castle

N o r t h

S e a

pigs

shamrock

IRELAND

□ **Dublin**

harp

UNITED

sheep

KINGDOM

Tower Bridge

rugby

windmills

NETHERLANDS

Amsterdam □
The Hague □

□ **London**

Gouda cheese

R. Rhine

G E

English Channel

A t l a n t i c
O c e a n

□ **Brussels**

BELGIUM

Frankfur

LUXEMBOURG

□

Luxembourg

Mont St Michel

R. Loire

Paris □

Arc de Triomphe

Eiffel Tower

R. Seine

owl

seafood

Bay of Biscay

F R A N C E

croissants

Bern

SWITZERLAND

Massif Central

I T A

26

⑤ ④ ③ ② ①

Arctic Ocean

blue whale

puffin

eider duck

owl

Lappland

Kola Peninsula

reindeer

wild mushrooms

fishing through ice

lemming

White Sea

wheat farming

R. Northern Dvina

moose

paper making

R. Sukhona

lynx

FINLAND

Gulf of Bothnia

Lake Onega

RUSSIAN

skiing

saunas

Lake Ladoga

St Petersburg

beavers

wild horses

Oslo

Helsinki

Winter Palace

FEDERATION

Vänern

Stockholm

Tallinn

Vättern

ESTONIA

dairy cows

Moscow

badger

LATVIA

Volga Uplands

Riga

R. Dvina

Kremlin

RK

Baltic Sea

Plain

Copenhagen

LITHUANIA

Central Russian

Vilnius

potatoes

R. Dnieper

RUS. FED.

wind farms

Minsk

North

European

R. Elbe

R. Vistula

BELARUS

Uplands

Berlin

Warsaw

boar

Russian dolls

It's a fact

POLAND

glass making

brown bears

Glass is made from sand. The sand is heated to a high temperature until it melts. Many items we use every day are made from glass. It is transparent - we can see through it. Sometimes metals are added to glass to change its colour. Brightly coloured stained glass is often found in church windows.

ANY

football

Prague

UKRAINE

CZECH REPUBLIC

R. Dniester

SLOVAKIA

Carpathian Mts

MOLDOVA

Bratislava

Munich

Vienna

R. Danube

Budapest

Chisinau

castle

AUSTRIA

HUNGARY

castle

ROMANIA

D

E

F

27

Southern Europe

⑤ ④ ③ ② ①

N W E S

DENMARK

North Sea

Hamburg

UNITED KINGDOM

NETHERLANDS
Amsterdam
The Hague

Hannover

Berlin

London

R. Rhine

GERMANY

Brussels

BELGIUM

Cologne

Frankfurt

English Channel

LUXEMBOURG

R. Seine

Atlantic Ocean

Paris

Eiffel Tower

Swiss cheese

cas

apples

R. Loire

Arc de Triomphe

football

seafood

FRANCE

croissants

grapes

Munich

Bay of Biscay

cheese

Bern

LIECHTENSTEIN

AU

wine

Massif Central

R. Rhône

SWITZERLAND

gondola

swordfish

Cantabrian Mts

garlic

skiing

Mont Blanc

cathedral

Milan

R. Po

Oporto

bull fighting

skiing

ANDORRA

Marseille

MONACO

Apennines

cars

SAN MAR

PORTUGAL

Spanish guitar

Madrid

Pyrenees

casinos

Leaning Tower of Pisa

Lisbon

R. Tagus

SPAIN

Barcelona

port

Rome

Vati

leather goods

beaches

cruise ships

Sardinia

Colosseum

sardines

oranges

flamenco dancers

almonds

Balearic Islands

grapes

Tyrrhenian Sea

Strait of Gibraltar

M e d i t e r

Sici

MOROCCO

ALGERIA

TUNISIA

The south of this region lies on the shores of the warm Mediterranean Sea where many people spend their holidays. Southern Europe and Africa are separated by only 15 kilometres (9 miles) of water known as the Strait of Gibraltar, which links the Atlantic Ocean and the Mediterranean Sea. Two of the world's smallest countries, Vatican City and Monaco, are in Southern Europe.

A F R

Ⓐ Ⓑ Ⓒ

It's a fact

A gondola is a traditional, long, narrow rowing boat used for transport on the canals in Venice. It is made from 8 different types of wood and is always painted black. Only one oar is used to push a gondola forward in the water.

Warsaw

P O L A N D

cathedral

Kiev

U K R A I N E

rague
**CZECH
EPUBLIC**

glass making

brown bears

R. Dniester

MOLDOVA

Carpathian Mts

enna
SLOVAKIA
Bratislava

HUNGARY

A

Budapest

Chisinau

SLOVENIA
jubljana
Zagreb

Hungarian church

castle

ROATIA

R O M A N I A

Croatian house
Belgrade

Bucharest

*Black
Sea*

**BOSNIA-
HERZEGOVINA**

R. Danube

roses

Sarajevo

Balkan Mts

SERBIA

MONTENEGRO

Sofia

grapes

driatic Sea

Podgorica

Skopje

BULGARIA

Istanbul

Tirana
ALBANIA

MACEDONIA

pizza

fortress

ples

Greek pottery

GREECE

Izmir

T U R K E Y

aghetti

olives

Greek church

*Aegean
Sea*

kebabs

Athens

volcano

*Ionian
Sea*

Parthenon

alletta

Cretan mosque

Crete

LTA

fishing boats

Knossos

n

e

a

n

S

e

a

L I B Y A

E G Y P T

I C A

D

E

F

Did you know?

• The islands of Sicily and Sardinia belong to Italy.

• Venice is built on a large area of water, called a lagoon.

• In Albania and Bulgaria nodding your head means no. Shaking your head from side to side means yes.

• In France April Fool's Day is known as April Fish Day.

• Portugal has the world's largest solar powered electricity plant.

• The wristwatch was invented in Switzerland.

• The River Danube flows through 7 countries.

What am I?

• I am made from flour, and egg or water.

• I am cooked quickly in boiling water.

• I am often covered in tomato sauce.

• My name means 'thin string'.

• I am a type of pasta.

What am I?

Answers at the back of the atlas.

Try this!

Many famous buidings and ruins are found in this region.
Look at the map and find

Arc de Triomphe
Colosseum
Knossos
Parthenon
Leaning Tower of Pisa

Asia

⑤

Asia is the largest continent. It is bigger than Europe and Africa combined. Asia extends from the Ural mountains to the Pacific Ocean in the east and from the Arctic Ocean to the Indian Ocean in the south. Climates vary from the cold Arctic in the north to hot tropical in the south.

A r c t i c

N

W ⊕ E

S

RUSSIAN FEDERATION

□ **Moscow**

E U R O P E

Ural Mountains

S   i

④

Black Sea

CYPRUS

Ankara □

Astana □

KAZAKHSTAN

GEORGIA

TURKEY

T'bilisi

LEBANON

Yerevan

□ AZERBAIJAN

Baku □

UZBEKISTAN

ISRAEL

SYRIA

ARMENIA

Caspian Sea

TURKMENISTAN

Bishkek

KYRGYZSTAN

□ **Damascus**

Amman □

Baghdad □

Ashgabat

Tashkent □

③

JORDAN

IRAQ

Tehran □

Dushanbe □

TAJIKISTAN

Kunlun Shan

BAHRAIN

Kuwait

KUWAIT

IRAN

AFGHANISTAN

Kabul □

Islamabad □

Plateau of Tibet

SAUDI ARABIA

Riyadh □

The Gulf

New Delhi □

NEPAL

Kathmandu □

Mount Everest ▲

BHUTAN

Thimphu

QATAR

UNITED ARAB EMIRATES

Muscat □

PAKISTAN

H i m a l a y a

Red Sea

Dhaka

A F R I C A

San'a □

OMAN

INDIA

BANGLADESH

MYANMAR (BURMA)

Naypyido

②

YEMEN

Socotra (Yemen)

A r a b i a n S e a

Bay of Bengal

Yango (Rango

Try this!

This country is also an island. Can you name it?

Andaman Is (India)

SRI LANKA

Nicobar Is (India)

Sri Jayewardenepura Kotte

MALDIVES

①   Answers at the back of the atlas.

I n d i a n   O c e a n

Ⓐ   Ⓑ   Ⓒ

Ocean

Bering Sea

Sea of Okhotsk

Lake Baikal

Ulan Bator

b e r i a

MONGOLIA

NORTH KOREA

Pyongyang

Beijing

Seoul

Sea of Japan (East Sea)

JAPAN

Tokyo

CHINA

SOUTH KOREA

East China Sea

Chang Jiang

T'aipei

TAIWAN

Pacific

Ocean

Hanoi

LAOS

Vientiane

South China Sea

Manila

PALAU

Melekeok

Bangkok

CAMBODIA

PHILIPPINES

Phnom Penh

VIETNAM

BRUNEI

THAILAND

Kuala Lumpur

MALAYSIA

Bandar Seri Begawan

Singapore

Borneo

Putrajaya

SINGAPORE

INDONESIA

EAST TIMOR

Jakarta

Dili

O C E A N I A

D   E   F

People facts

- Population: 4 085 000 000 (including Russian Federation)

- Country with most people: China 1 323 345 000

- City with most people: Tokyo 35 327 000

Geography facts

- Area: 45 036 492 square kilometres (17 388 686 square miles)

- Largest country: Russian Federation 17 075 400 square kilometres (6 592 849 square miles)

- Longest river: Chang Jiang 6380 kilometres (3964 miles)

- Highest mountain: Mount Everest 8848 metres (29 028 feet)

- Largest lake: Caspian Sea 371 000 square kilometres (143 243 square miles)

- Largest island: Borneo 745 561 square kilometres (287 863 square miles)

Did you know?

- More than half of the world's people live in Asia.

- Lake Baikal, in Siberia, is the deepest lake in the world.

- The Chinese invented paper, ink, the compass and silk.

- Indonesia has more active volcanoes than any other country.

- The Dead Sea is so salty bathers can float on top of the water.

- The Siberian tiger is the largest living cat in the world.

- The red dot in the centre of the Japanese flag represents a red sun.

Russian Federation

⑤

Russia is the largest country in the world. It has borders with 14 different countries. Most Russians live in the west of the country. Siberia, in the north, is almost empty. It is dry and extremely cold there. The southwest, on the coast of the Black Sea, is very warm. Much of the country is covered with huge grassy plains, known as steppes.

Barents Sea

FINLAND

Baltic Sea

ESTONIA

reindeer

fishing in the Arctic

Kara Sea

④ **POLAND**

potatoes

RUS. FED.

LITHUANIA

LATVIA

St Petersburg

ice hockey

□ **Archangel**

eider duck

vodka

BELARUS

gymnastics

Kremlin

R. North Dvina

R. Pechora

Ural owl

□ **Vorkuta**

lynx

S i b

R. Yenisey

R. Dniestr

Kiev
UKRAINE

□ **Moscow**

Nizhniy Novgorod ○

ballet

Mountains

R. Ob

R U S S I A

R. Lower Tunguska

③ football

Kazan

Perm

F E D E R A T

MOLDOVA

R. Dnieper

Sea of Azou

sugarbeet

R. Don

R. Volga

wheat

Yekaterinburg
Samara ○

Ufa

chess

cathedral

Ural

West

Siberian

Plain

R. Yenisey

Volgograd

Chelyabinsk

Cossack dancers

□ **Omsk**

brown bear

Black Sea

balalaika

Russian dolls

cathedral

Novosibirsk ○

Krasnoyarsk

TURKEY

GEORGIA

Caspian seal

K A Z A K H S T A N

□ **Astana**

② **ARMENIA**

AZ. AZERBAIJAN

Caspian Sea

Aral Sea

Siberian stag

U Z B E K I S T A N

rocket launch site

R. Syrdarya

Lake Balkhash

I R A N

T U R K M E N I S T A N

wheat

M O N G O

① **Ashgabat** □

R. Amudarya

Tashkent □

□ **Bishkek**

KYRGYZSTAN

TAJIKISTAN

Ⓐ **AFGHANISTAN** Ⓑ

C **H**

Ⓒ

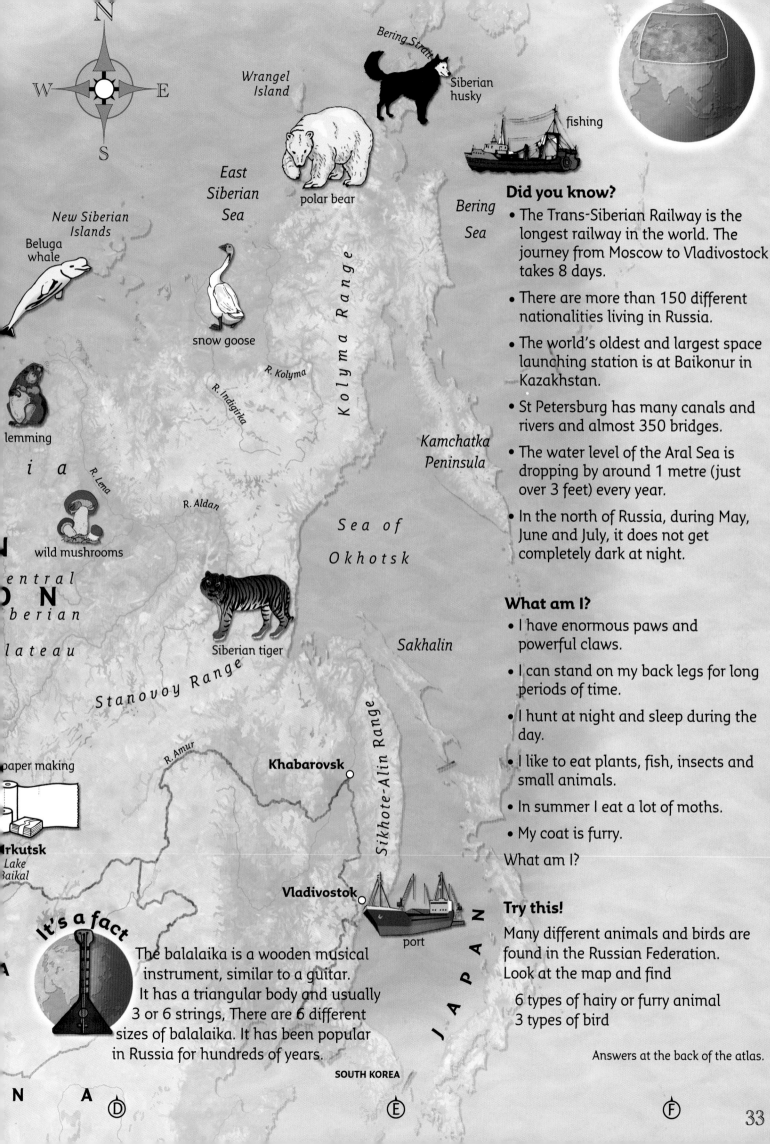

N W E S

Bering Strait

Wrangel Island

Siberian husky

East Siberian Sea

polar bear

New Siberian Islands

Beluga whale

Bering Sea

fishing

snow goose

R. Kolyma

R. Indigirka

Kolyma Range

lemming

i a

R. Lena

R. Aldan

wild mushrooms

Kamchatka Peninsula

Sea of Okhotsk

entral

ON

berian

lateau

Siberian tiger

Sakhalin

Stanovoy Range

R. Amur

Sikhote-Alin Range

paper making

Khabarovsk

rkutsk

Lake Baikal

Vladivostok

port

It's a fact

The balalaika is a wooden musical instrument, similar to a guitar. It has a triangular body and usually 3 or 6 strings, There are 6 different sizes of balalaika. It has been popular in Russia for hundreds of years.

J A P A N

SOUTH KOREA

N A D E F

Did you know?

- The Trans-Siberian Railway is the longest railway in the world. The journey from Moscow to Vladivostock takes 8 days.

- There are more than 150 different nationalities living in Russia.

- The world's oldest and largest space launching station is at Baikonur in Kazakhstan.

- St Petersburg has many canals and rivers and almost 350 bridges.

- The water level of the Aral Sea is dropping by around 1 metre (just over 3 feet) every year.

- In the north of Russia, during May, June and July, it does not get completely dark at night.

What am I?

- I have enormous paws and powerful claws.

- I can stand on my back legs for long periods of time.

- I hunt at night and sleep during the day.

- I like to eat plants, fish, insects and small animals.

- In summer I eat a lot of moths.

- My coat is furry.

What am I?

Try this!

Many different animals and birds are found in the Russian Federation. Look at the map and find

6 types of hairy or furry animal
3 types of bird

Answers at the back of the atlas.

Southwest Asia

RUSSIA

Black Sea

GREECE

El'brus

GEORGI

The north and west of this area is mountainous, with high ranges extending through Turkey into Iran. The Arabian Peninsula between the Red Sea and The Gulf is mostly dry sandy desert. Water is scarce in much of Southwest Asia. Two major rivers are the Tigris and Euphrates.

kebabs

□ **Ankara**

mosque

coffee

ARMEN

Yereva

Taurus Mts

T U R K E Y

Crusader castles

cedar trees

Nicosia □

CYPRUS

Mediterranean Sea

SYRIA

date palms

Beirut

LEBANON □

ISRAEL □ **Damascus**

Baghda

R.

R. Euphrates

Amman

□ □ **JORDAN**

Jerusalem

Syrian Desert

oil refineries

IRA

Did you know?

- Saudi Arabia is the world's leading exporter of oil.

- Three of the world's major religions started in this area: Judaism, Christianity and Islam.

- Damascus, the capital of Syria, is one of the oldest cities in the world.

- The Caucasus mountain range protects Armenia, Georgia and Azerbaijan from cold north winds.

Cairo

Sphinx

L I B Y A

Dome of the Rock

Arabian fox *A n   N a f u d*

carpets

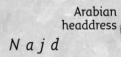

Bedouin tent

R. Nile

desert safari

Arabian headdress

N a j d

Riyad

What am I?

- I am a type of bird.
- I have long, thin legs and a long neck.
- I like to wade in shallow water.
- I often stand on one leg.
- I eat small shrimps.
- I am pink.

What am I?

E G Y P T

scuba diving

Muslim praying at Mecca

S A U D

crocodile

R. Nile

angel fish

A

s

i

r

Arabian hors

R

e

d

S

e

a

Try this!

Look at the map. Can you find these:

3 Arabian animals
1 religious building
1 sport popular in Pakistan

Answers at the back of the atlas.

S U D A N

dhow

San'a □

YE

E

R

I

T

R

E

A

Ras Dejen

⑤
④
③
②
①

Ⓐ

Ⓑ

E T H I O P I A

Ⓒ **DJIBOUTI**

G u

FEDERATION

Caspian seal

skiing

Caucasus

Caspian
Sea

T'bilisi

AZERBAIJAN

Baku

ER.

carpets

oil rig

flamingo

N

W   E

S

*Aral
Sea*

space
station

R. Sydar'ya

wheat

KAZAKHSTAN

Tashkent

KYRGYZSTAN

CHINA

TURKMENISTAN

R. Amudar'ya

TAJIKISTAN

Dushanbe

jackal

Elburz Mts

Tehran

onager

Ashgabat

Hindu Kush

Karakoram Range

Kabul

Islamabad

AFGHANISTAN

R. Indus

mosque

I   R   A   N

Zagros Mountains

Afghan hounds

Sikh

KUWAIT

Kuwait

The Gulf

PAKISTAN

R. Indus

Thar Desert

BAHRAIN

Manama

QATAR

Doha

OMAN

Gulf of Oman

Karachi

cricket

INDIA

oil wells

Abu Dhabi

UNITED ARAB
EMIRATES

Muscat

Mouths of
the Indus

ARABIA

Arabian
camel

oryx

O   M   A   N

oil tankers

*Arabian
Sea*

Rub' al Khali

date palms

octopus

date palms

Arabian
fishing boats

dates

great white
shark

green turtle

of Oman

It's a fact

The oryx is a type of antelope.
with long, straight horns.
The oryx became extinct in the
Arabian Peninsula in the 1970s.
It has been re-introduced but it is
being hunted for its horn. This animal
can live in the desert without water for
long periods.

Ⓓ   Ⓔ   Ⓕ   35

South Asia

⑦ South Asia is a region of contrasting landscapes and weather. In the north is the great mountain range of Himalaya where the climate is harsh and few people live. The lands at the mouths of the Ganges river are low lying and flooding occurs during the heavy rains in the monsoon season. Most people live in the river valleys, plains and big cities.

N
W E
S

What am I?
- I live in the sea, especially around coral reefs.
- I have 3 hearts and my blood is blue.
- My soft body means that I can squeeze through small spaces.
- I have a beak.
- I have 8 arms.

What am I?

Try this!

Many different animals, birds and fish are found in this region. Look at the map and find

3 members of the cat family
2 types of bird
1 type of animal with sharp spines

Answers at the back of the atlas.

C H I N A

K u n l u n   S h a n

P l a t e a u   o f   T i b e t

H i m a l a y a

Lhasa

Tibetan monks

Thimphu
BHUTAN

Mount Everest

Patna

⑥ TAJIKISTAN

□ Dushanbe

jackal

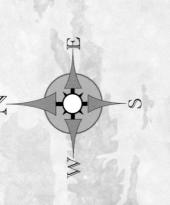
snow leopard

K2

Kashmir stag

H i n d u   K u s h

mountain goat

Kabul □

□ Islamabad

AFGHANISTAN

Lahore ○

Faisalabad ○

⑤ P A K I S T A N

Afghan hound

T h a r   D e s e r t

Sikh

R. Indus

Golden Temple, Amritsar

Delhi □
New Delhi □

Jaipur ○

Taj Mahal

yak

R. Brahmaputra

N E P A L

Kathmandu □

Nepalese temple

Indian rhinoceros

R. Gan

BANGLADESH

elephants

INDIA

Karachi

cricket

Ahmadabad

Asiatic lion

Indore

Bhopal

peacock

hockey

Pune

Mumbai

port

Arabian Sea

octopus

Nagpur

R. Godavari

Indian porcupine

rickshaw

Hyderabad

Vijayawada

Eastern Ghats

Western Ghats

Deccan

Bangalore

Chennai

sitar

Trivandrum

Buddhism

MALDIVES

Maldive anemonefish

coral reefs

Bhopal

Bay of Bengal

Dhaka

rice

Chittagong

Mandalay

MYANMAR
(BURMA)

R. Irrawaddy

seafood

Andaman Is *(India)*

Nicobar Is *(India)*

parakeet

Kolkata

Mouths of the Ganges

tiger

It's a fact

The sitar is a traditional string instrument with a distinctive sound. It has been popular in India and the surrounding countries for hundreds of years. The body of a sitar is made from a gourd. The neck is made from wood. There can be between 18 and 20 strings. It is a difficult instrument to learn to play.

tea

Sri Jayewardenepura Kotte

SRI LANKA

Indian Ocean

Did you know?

- The island of Sri Lanka is famous for growing tea.

- There are more than 25 tiger reserves in India, where the animals are protected.

- 8 of the world's 10 highest mountains are in Nepal.

- The Nepalese flag is not rectangular – it is shaped from 2 triangles.

- Many Indian temples own elephants. The animals are decorated and used in religious festivals.

Ⓐ Ⓑ Ⓒ Ⓓ

① ② ③

37

China and Japan

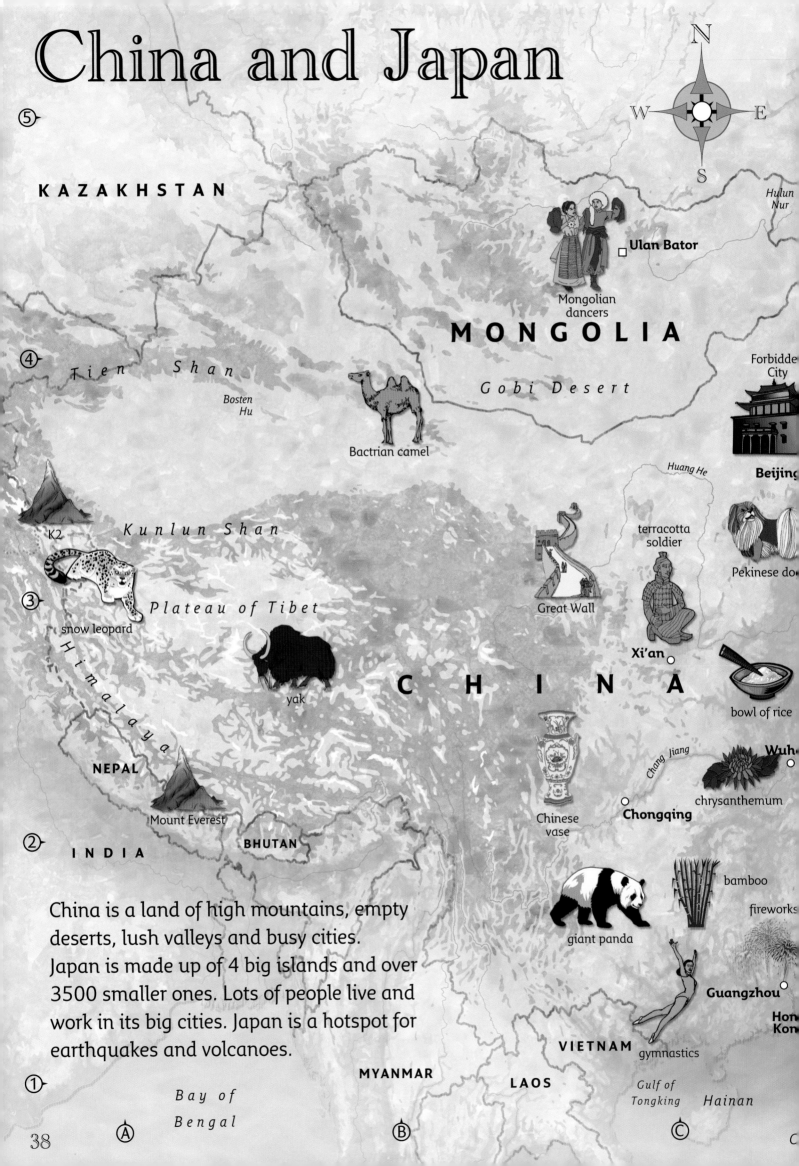

⑤

KAZAKHSTAN

Hulun Nur

Mongolian dancers

□ **Ulan Bator**

MONGOLIA

④

Tien   Shan

Bosten Hu

Gobi Desert

Forbidde City

Bactrian camel

Huang He

Beijing

K2

Kunlun Shan

terracotta soldier

Great Wall

Pekinese do

③

Plateau of Tibet

snow leopard

Himalaya

yak

C H I N A

Xi'an ○

bowl of rice

Chinese vase

Chang Jiang

Wuh

chrysanthemum

NEPAL

Mount Everest

BHUTAN

Chongqing ○

②

INDIA

China is a land of high mountains, empty deserts, lush valleys and busy cities. Japan is made up of 4 big islands and over 3500 smaller ones. Lots of people live and work in its big cities. Japan is a hotspot for earthquakes and volcanoes.

bamboo

fireworks

giant panda

Guangzhou ○

Hon Kon

VIETNAM

gymnastics

①

MYANMAR

LAOS

Gulf of Tongking *Hainan*

38

Ⓐ

Bay of Bengal

Ⓑ

Ⓒ

RUSSIAN FEDERATION

sperm whale
Sea of Okhotsk

skiing

Sapporo

JAPAN

bonsai tree

kites

Harbin

Lake Khanka

Shenyang

Sea of Japan (East Sea)

NORTH KOREA

karate

Buddhist monk
ianjin

Pyongyang

Korea Bay

Tokyo

Honshu

girl in kimono

Seoul

SOUTH KOREA

sumo wrestling

electronics industry

Yellow Sea

rice growing

car industry

bullet train

rickshaw

Sakura-jima

tea

Shanghai

East China Sea

puffer fish

chopsticks

Ryukyu Islands

Chinese junk

T'aipei

octopus

pagoda

TAIWAN

tuna

port

Pacific Ocean

PHILIPPINES

uth a Sea

D

E

Did you know?

• Gunpowder was first discovered in China. It can be used to make fireworks and signal flares.

• Chinese is spoken by almost a quarter of all the people in the world.

• China is one of the few countries where fossils of 'Big Foot' (homo gigantus) have been found.

• In Japan the green traffic light is called 'blue'.

• Japan has about 1500 earthquakes each year.

What am I?

• I am made of baked earth.

• My purpose was to protect the first Emperor in the afterlife.

• I was buried in 210-109 BC.

• I was discovered in 1974.

• I belonged to an army.

What am I?

Try this!

China has many different animals. Look at the map and find

The big furry animal who loves to eat bamboo.

Many sports are played in Japan

Can you name 2 of these?

Answers at the back of the atlas.

It's a fact

The giant panda has lived in bamboo forests for several million years. Each year a panda can eat 5 tonnes of bamboo. There are only about 1600 left in the wild.

Southeast Asia

CHINA

Taiwan Strait

TAIWAN

⑤ **MYANMAR (BURMA)**

Naypyidaw □

Bay of Bengal

R. Irrawaddy

R. Salween

rubies

temple

Yangon (Rangoon) □

Hanoi □

Buddhist monk

Vientiane □

L A O S

V I E T N A M

R. Mekong

Hainan

satellite launch centre

Luzo

Pinatubo – volca

Manilo

python

THAILAND

Angkor Wat

South China Sea

seafood

④

chili peppers

Bangkok □

CAMBODIA

Phnom Penh □

rice growing

Sulu Sea

Andaman Sea

scuba diving

Gulf of Thailand

oil rig

beaches

③

Strait of Malacca

Kuala Lumpur □

Putrajaya □

Sumatra tiger

M A L A Y S I A

sky scrapers

Singapore □ **SINGAPORE**

BRUNEI □ **Bandar Seri Begawan**

Cel S

rubber trees

Borneo

Macassar Strait

coral reefs

Sumatra

rhinoceros

orang utan

water buffa

Celeb

② *Indian Ocean*

Java Sea

temple

Jakarta □

I N D O N

Java

Balinese mask

Flores S

Southeast Asia is made up of a tropical mainland peninsula, sometimes called Indo-China, and over 20 000 islands. Much of the region is rainforest which has a huge variety of wildlife such as elephants, tigers, orang utans and rhinoceros.

volcano

Komodo dragon

surfing

① 40

Ⓐ

Ⓑ

Ⓒ

tuna

N
W **E**
S

Pacific

Ocean

rait

uzon

It's a fact

Many rubber tree plantations are found in Southeast Asia. When rubber trees are 5-6 years old they produce latex, collected from slits made in the tree trunk. Latex is made into rubber. The trees produce latex for 20-25 years. They are then cut down and the wood is used to make furniture.

PHILIPPINES

oyster and pearl

Mindanao

pineapples

e s

clams

Molucca Sea

coral reefs

coconut
palm tree

□ **Melekeok**

PALAU

manta
ray

cowrie shell

New
Guinea

Puncak Jaya

E S I A
Banda Sea

Dili
□ **EAST**
TIMOR

Arafura
Sea

rubber trees

PAPUA NEW

GUINEA

Did you know?

• Singapore is made up of 63 islands.

• The western half of New Guinea is part of Indonesia.

• There are around 150 active volcanoes in Indonesia.

• The Sumatran tiger is the smallest tiger. It is a very fast swimmer.

• A cowrie is the shell of a snail that lives in the sea in tropical areas.

What am I?

• I am a type of lizard.

• I am only found in central Indonesia.

• I have a long body, sharp teeth and strong claws.

• My tongue is long and yellow.

• I am sometimes known as a dragon.

What am I?

Try this!

2 water sports are shown on the map. Can you name them?

Answers at the back of the atlas.

A U S T R A L I A

Coral
Sea

Ⓓ Ⓔ Ⓕ

Oceania

⑤

N

W   E

S

INDONESIA

Puncak Jaya ▲

New Guinea

PAPUA NEW GUINEA

Solomon Sea

A r a f u r a   S e a

Port Moresby

Honiare

④

Timor Sea   ○ **Darwin**

Gulf of Carpentaria

C o r a l   S e a

I n d i a n   O c e a n

Great Barrier Reef

Great Sandy Desert

AUSTRALIA

Great Dividing Range

Brisbane ○

③

Great Victoria Desert

Lake Eyre

R. Darling

Dividing Range

Perth ○

Great Australian Bight

Adelaide ○

R. Murray

Sydney ○

□ **Canberra**

Great

Melbourne ○

T a s m a n   S e a

Tasmania

②

Hobart ○

Oceania is the smallest continent and lies within the
tropics. It is made up of the countries of Australia, New
Zealand, Papua New Guinea and over 20 000 small Pacific
islands. Australia is by far the largest country and the
majority of the population live on the coast. The central
region of the country is a vast desert known as the outback.
New Zealand is mountainous with a temperate climate and
Papua New Guinea is mainly rainforest.

①

Ⓐ   Ⓑ   Ⓒ

Bairiki

Yaren

NAURU

KIRIBATI

SOLOMON
ISLANDS

TUVALU

Vaiaku

VANUATU

Wallis and
Futuna Islands
(France)

SAMOA

Port Vila

Apia

American
Samoa
(USA)

New
Caledonia
(France)

Nouméa

Suva

TONGA

Niue
(New
Zealand)

FIJI

Nuku'alofa

Cook
Islands
(New
Zealand)

FRENCH
POLYNESIA

P a c i f i c

O c e a n

Auckland

NEW
ZEALAND

*North
Island*

Wellington

*South
Island*

Did you know?

- 40% of Australia is covered by sand dunes.

- Australia's Great Barrier Reef is the world's largest coral reef.

- In South Island, New Zealand, there are 18 peaks of more than 3000 metres (9842 feet).

- The stars on the flags of Oceanic countries represent the Southern Cross constellation.

- Kangaroos are only found in Australia and New Guinea but there are over 40 different types.

People facts

- Population: 33 000 000

- Country with most people: Australia 20 155 000

- City with most people: Sydney 4 388 000

Geography facts

- Area: 8 844 516 square kilometres (3 414 887 square miles)

- Largest country: Australia 7 692 024 square kilometres (2 969 907 square miles)

- Longest river: Murray-Darling 3750 kilometres (2330 miles)

- Highest mountain: Puncak Jaya 5030 metres (16 502 feet)

- Largest lake: Lake Eyre 0-8900 square kilometres (0-3436 square miles)

- Largest island: New Guinea 808 510 square kilometres (312 167 square miles)

Try this!

Which countries do these flags belong to?

Answers at the back of the atlas.

D   E   F   43

Australia & New Zealand

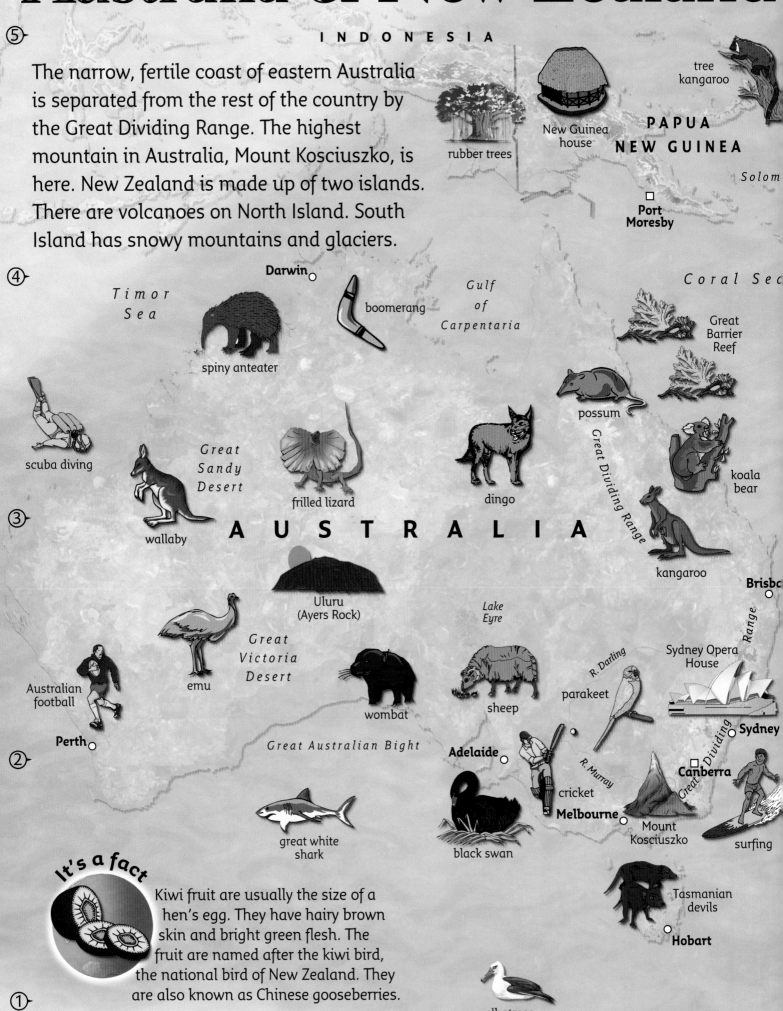

INDONESIA

The narrow, fertile coast of eastern Australia is separated from the rest of the country by the Great Dividing Range. The highest mountain in Australia, Mount Kosciuszko, is here. New Zealand is made up of two islands. There are volcanoes on North Island. South Island has snowy mountains and glaciers.

tree kangaroo

rubber trees

New Guinea house

PAPUA NEW GUINEA

Solom

Port Moresby

⑤

④

Timor Sea

Darwin

boomerang

Gulf of Carpentaria

Coral Sea

Great Barrier Reef

spiny anteater

scuba diving

Great Sandy Desert

frilled lizard

dingo

possum

Great Dividing Range

koala bear

③

wallaby

A U S T R A L I A

kangaroo

Brisb

Uluru (Ayers Rock)

Lake Eyre

Range

emu

Great Victoria Desert

wombat

sheep

R. Darling

parakeet

Sydney Opera House

Australian football

Perth

②

Great Australian Bight

Adelaide

cricket

R. Murray

Melbourne

Canberra

Sydney

Mount Kosciuszko

Great Dividing

surfing

great white shark

black swan

It's a fact

Kiwi fruit are usually the size of a hen's egg. They have hairy brown skin and bright green flesh. The fruit are named after the kiwi bird, the national bird of New Zealand. They are also known as Chinese gooseberries.

Tasmanian devils

Hobart

albatross

①

44

Ⓐ

Ⓑ

Ⓒ

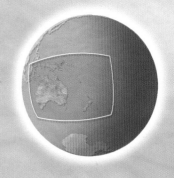

cuscus

flying fish

N A U R U

☐ Yaren

K I R I B A T I

a

Honiara ☐

S O L O M O N
I S L A N D S

clown
fish

T U V A L U

What am I?

- I have powerful back legs, large feet, and use my long tail for balance.
- I like to eat grass and roots.
- I live in groups called mobs.
- As a baby, I live in my mother's pouch.
- I hop around, sometimes very fast.

What am I?

Answers at the back of the atlas.

V A N U A T U

coconut
palms

S A M O A

Apia ☐

coconuts

☐ **Port Vila**

F I J I

bananas

New Caledonia
(France)

☐ **Nouméa**

☐ **Suva**

rugby

TONGA

Nuku'alofa ☐

sea horses

octopus

swordfish

P a c i f i c   O c e a n

Try this!

There are many kinds of birds and sea creatures in this region. Look at the map and find

1 black bird
4 types of sea creature

Answers at the back of the atlas.

barracudas

kiwi

Auckland ○

rugby

volcanoes

kiwi
fruit

Wellington ☐

T a s m a n
S e a

NEW
ZEALAND

sheep   takahe

Did you know?

- This region is on the opposite side of the world to Europe.
- It takes 3 days and 3 nights to cross Australia by train, from Perth to Sydney.
- On South Island, New Zealand, there are more sheep than people.
- There is natural hot steam underground on North Island. The steam is used to produce electricity.
- There are more than 850 native languages used in Papua New Guinea.

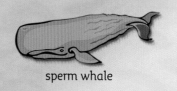
sperm whale

Ⓓ   Ⓔ   Ⓕ   45

The Arctic Ocean

The Arctic Ocean is at the North Pole. Much of the sea is covered in ice all year round. It is the smallest and shallowest ocean in the world.

Try this!

Look at the map and find

1 type of air transport
1 type of water transport
1 type of land transport

Answers at the back of the atlas.

Bering Sea

walrus

Siberian husky

Kolyma Range

polar bear

snow goose

Wrangel Island

East Siberian Sea

Siberian tiger

caribou

Brooks Range

NORTH AMERICA

Verkhoyansk Range

ringed seal

Arctic fox

ice breaker ship

Arctic terns

ski plane

lynx

Arctic snow mobile

Arctic hare

Arctic Ocean

Central Siberian Plateau

musk ox

Parry Islands

Severnaya Zemlya

North Pole

Arctic explorer

lemming

kayak

Ellesmere Island

ASIA

Baffin Island

Baffin Bay

polar bear

Franz Josef Land

Kara Sea

ptarmigan

igloo

Arctic communications satellite

Novaya Zemlya

reindeer

Spitzbergen

Greenland

Barents Sea

Inuit

killer whale

Scandinavia

Iceland

iceberg

Norwegian Sea

EUROPE

It's a fact

The Inuit are a group of people native to the coasts of the Arctic Ocean. They have lived there for over 1000 years. Inuit are hunters and fishermen. Mostly they hunt caribou and seal. Inuit fish from boats called kayaks, a type of canoe. They travel across the snow and ice on sledges pulled by teams of dogs. Their language, Inukitut, uses symbols instead of letters.

Did you know?

• The permanent ice of the Arctic Ocean is about 4 metres (13 feet) thick.

• The Arctic is the least salty of all the oceans.

• It never rains in the Arctic Ocean – it only snows.

Antarctica

Antarctica is the area of thick ice surrounding the South Pole. It is the coldest, windiest and driest continent.

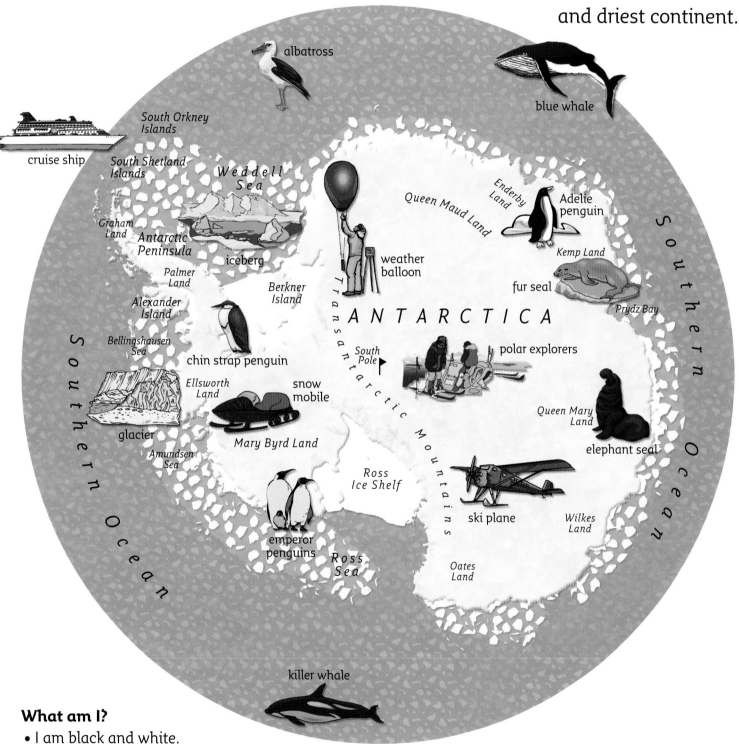

albatross

blue whale

cruise ship

South Orkney Islands

South Shetland Islands

Weddell Sea

Graham Land

Antarctic Peninsula

iceberg

Palmer Land

Berkner Island

Alexander Island

Bellingshausen Sea

chin strap penguin

glacier

Ellsworth Land

snow mobile

Mary Byrd Land

Amundsen Sea

emperor penguins

Ross Ice Shelf

Ross Sea

killer whale

Southern Ocean

weather balloon

Queen Maud Land

Enderby Land

Adelie penguin

Kemp Land

fur seal

Prydz Bay

ANTARCTICA

South Pole ▶

polar explorers

Transantarctic Mountains

Queen Mary Land

elephant seal

ski plane

Wilkes Land

Oates Land

Southern Ocean

What am I?

- I am black and white.
- I eat fish and other sea life.
- I spend half my life on land and half in the sea.
- I am an excellent swimmer.
- On land I waddle on my feet, or slide on my tummy.
- I have wings but cannot fly.

What am I?

Answers at the back of the atlas.

Did you know?

- No one country owns Antarctica.
- No one lives permanently in Antarctica. Scientists visit to learn about the area.
- Many features on Antarctica are named after explorers.

Where have you been?

This world map shows some of the most visited countries in the world. You may have also visited some of these places. Perhaps you spent a holiday or visited friends and relations in these countries.

Look at the comments from children who have spent some time travelling in far away places. Would you agree with their comments or have you more interesting stories to tell?

Barcelona
Barcelona has lots of great shops and the weather is brilliant. It has lots of beaches.
Sophie 10 years

Greece
It's really hot and has lots of outdoor swimming pools and all the times I've been there there's been some really cute cats.
Vicki 10 years

Scotland
I really like the lochs, mountains and forests. The history is definitely the best.
Jake 10 years

Australia
We built sand castles on the beach.
David 6 years

Spain
My favourite place is Salou in Spain because there is a huge theme park, Port Aventura.
Taylor 10 years

London
In London it is very cold in the winter. My Gran lives there. I love London.
Jasmin 10 years

Czech Republic
The Czech Republic is a beautiful place. I visit there with my Gran to see my cousins.
Isaac 10 years

Top 10 countries visited
1. France
2. Spain
3. United States of America
4. China
5. Italy
6. United Kingdom
7. Mexico
8. Germany
9. Turkey
10. Austria

Turkey
The food was nice, especially the lovely cherries from the market near Bodrum! We saw camels and I had a ride on one of them. The best thing was doing back flips on a bungee trampoline.
Charley 10 years

Slovakia
I really liked the snow and building a giant snowman, falling into the snow and skiing.
Marek 4 years

CANADA

UNITED STATES OF AMERICA

BERMUDA

MEXICO

What do you think?

France
I was in France whilst they were in the final of the World Cup. I got to stay up late and make as much noise as I could without being heard.
Calum 10 years

Portugal
I like the swimming pools outside.
Cain 10 years

France
I used to live in France. I will always have this memory. One day it went snowy, sun, snow, sun etc....
Cameron 10 years

GERMANY
UNITED KINGDOM
CZECH REP.
IRELAND
SLOVAKIA
FRANCE
AUSTRIA
ITALY
PORTUGAL
TURKEY
SPAIN
GREECE
CHINA
INDIA
KENYA
MALAYSIA
SOUTH AFRICA
AUSTRALIA
NEW ZEALAND

Scotland
The most exciting thing was when I was panning for gold at the Wanlockhead Lead Mine Museum and found some in the bottom of my pan.
Callum 8 years

Florida
We went to Disneyworld to see Mickey Mouse. It was very hot.
Brad 7 years

Majorca
It is famous because it has a Pirate Show. Its main place is Palma.
Ross 10 years

Scotland
My favourite place is Loch Lomond.
Jordan 10 years

Scotland
I went to Millport. It was thunder and lightning. It struck a lamppost and it fell down on the road.
Antonio 10 years

Scotland
Edinburgh Dungeons has the most scary weirdest monsters in the world. I got the monster stuck in my dreams.
Brian 10 years

Disneyland Paris
Disneyland was great. It was sad when I had to leave.
Daniel 10 years

Spain
I liked Majorca because of the sun and the price of shopping. It was also really good because of the big beaches.
Kieran 10 years

49

Where have you been?

There are many reasons to travel to far away places. The symbols around this map show a selection of these. Names on the map tell us some of the best places to visit.

More interesting stories are also shown.

Sightseeing

North America

Rocky Mountains

Winter sports

Beach holiday

Cruise

Caribbean Sea

S a

USA

I like Universal Studio because it has fantastic rides. I would give it a ten out of ten.

Sam 10 years

Kenya

We were in a big car and saw elephants and lions. I liked the lions but they had big teeth. It was very dusty and hot.

Katie 7 years

Bird watching

South America

Andes

Desert Safa

USA

I used to live in Vermont. In winter it snows a lot and in the summer it is very hot.

Aidan 10 years

India

India is the greatest place ever.

Naomi 10 years

Malaysia

We went to the jungle and saw lots of animals in the trees. I was scared because the animals made lots of noise at night. It was hot but it rained every day.

Kim 8 years

Exploring

A n t

Australia

I love Australia because of all the different animals on land and in the water and all of the lovely weather.

Robbie 10 years

Canary Islands

My favourite place is Tenerife because it's very comfortable...

Darren 10 years

Cadiz, Spain

My feet were almost burnt when I went on the beaches because the sand was so hot. Luckily the water cooled me down.

Helen 10 years

What do you think?

Turkey

It's really HOT!! I sleep walked into the hallway of our dormitory and I had nightmares about one of my Aunt's friend's cousins.

Sean 10 years

Scotland

Arran is an island off the southwest coast of Scotland. The funniest thing is when my friend catapults people across the bedroom with his feet. The best thing was when I got to ride a horse through a river on a pony trek.

Rona 10 years

South Africa

It was hot. We went on a boat and saw fish in the sea. I had a sore tummy in the boat.

Cameron 5 years

Greece

Rhodes in Greece is quiet with fantastic beaches.

Martha 10 years

Spain

My favourite city is Barcelona because it is very lively.

Megan 10 years

New Zealand

We made snowballs to throw at each other. But it was very cold.

Sophie 8 years

Asia

Himalaya

pe

nean Sea

r a

Africa

East Africa

Trekking

Australia

Water sports

Wildlife watching

ctica

Canada

I love Canada because of the cool stuff to see and it is only 1 hour away from Disneyland.

Makeila 10 years

USA

Florida is where I always go with my family. There are lots of things to do like rides and stuff.

Megan 10 years

Ireland

My Great Granny lives in Ireland. It has great restaurants.

Molly 10 years

Bermuda

Bermuda is always peaceful and quiet.

Callum 10 years

Barcelona

Barcelona has lots of great shops and the weather is brilliant. It has lots of beaches.

Sophie 10 years

Countries of the World

Flag	COUNTRY, CONTINENT / Capital City / Population	Area square kilometres (square miles)

AFGHANISTAN, ASIA
Kabul
29 863 000
652 225
(251 825)

ALBANIA, EUROPE
Tirana
3 130 000
28 748
(11 100)

ALGERIA, AFRICA
Algiers
32 854 000
2 381 741
(919 595)

ANGOLA, AFRICA
Luanda
15 941 000
1 246 700
(481 353)

ARGENTINA, SOUTH AMERICA
Buenos Aires
38 747 000
2 766 889
(1 068 302)

ARMENIA, ASIA
Yerevan
3 016 000
29 800
(11 506)

AUSTRALIA, OCEANIA
Canberra
20 155 000
7 692 024
(2 969 907)

AUSTRIA, EUROPE
Vienna
8 189 000
83 855
(32 377)

BAHRAIN, ASIA
Manama
727 000
691
(267)

BANGLADESH, ASIA
Dhaka
141 822 000
143 998
(55 598)

BELARUS, EUROPE
Minsk
9 755 000
207 600
(80 155)

BELGIUM, EUROPE
Brussels
10 419 000
30 520
(11 784)

BENIN, AFRICA
Porto Novo
8 439 000
112 620
(43 483)

BHUTAN, ASIA
Thimphu
2 163 000
46 620
(18 000)

BOLIVIA, SOUTH AMERICA
La Paz/Sucre
9 182 000
1 098 581
(424 164)

BOSNIA-HERZEGOVINA, EUROPE
Sarajevo
3 907 000
51 130
(19 741)

BOTSWANA, AFRICA
Gaborone
1 765 000
581 370
(224 468)

BRAZIL, SOUTH AMERICA
Brasília
186 405 000
8 514 879
(3 287 613)

BRUNEI, ASIA
Bandar Seri Begawan
374 000
5 765
(2 226)

BULGARIA, EUROPE
Sofia
7 726 000
110 994
(42 855)

BURKINA, AFRICA
Ouagadougou
13 228 000
274 200
(105 869)

BURUNDI, AFRICA
Bujumbura
7 548 000
27 835
(10 747)

CAMBODIA, ASIA
Phnom Penh
14 071 000
181 035
(69 884)

CAMEROON, AFRICA
Yaoundé
16 322 000
475 442
(183 569)

CANADA, NORTH AMERICA
Ottawa
32 268 000
9 984 670
(3 855 103)

CENTRAL AFRICAN REPUBLIC, AFRICA
Bangui
4 038 000
622 436
(240 324)

CHAD, AFRICA
Ndjamena
9 749 000
1 284 000
(495 755)

CHILE, SOUTH AMERICA
Santiago
16 295 000
756 945
(292 258)

CHINA, ASIA
Beijing
1 323 345 000
9 584 492
(3 700 593)

COLOMBIA, SOUTH AMERICA
Bogotá
45 600 000
1 141 748
(440 831)

CONGO, AFRICA
Brazzaville
3 999 000
342 000
(132 047)

CONGO, DEMOCRATIC REPUBLIC OF THE AFRICA
Kinshasa
57 549 000
2 345 410
(905 568)

COSTA RICA, NORTH AMERICA
San José
4 327 000
51 100
(19 730)

CÔTE D'IVOIRE, AFRICA
Yamoussoukro
18 154 000
322 463
(124 504)

CROATIA, EUROPE
Zagreb
4 551 000
56 538
(21 829)

CUBA, NORTH AMERICA
Havana
11 269 000
110 860
(42 803)

CYPRUS, ASIA
Nicosia
835 000
9 251
(3 572)

CZECH REPUBLIC, EUROPE
Prague
10 220 000
78 864
(30 450)

DENMARK, EUROPE
Copenhagen
5 431 000
43 075
(16 631)

DJIBOUTI, AFRICA
🏢 Djibouti
👥 793 000
✉ 23 200 (8 958)

DOMINICAN REPUBLIC, NORTH AMERICA
🏢 Santo Domingo
👥 8 895 000
✉ 48 442 (18 704)

EAST TIMOR, ASIA
🏢 Dili
👥 947 000
✉ 14 874 (5 743)

ECUADOR, SOUTH AMERICA
🏢 Quito
👥 13 228 000
✉ 272 045 (105 037)

EGYPT, AFRICA
🏢 Cairo
👥 74 033 000
✉ 1 000 250 (386 199)

EL SALVADOR, NORTH AMERICA
🏢 San Salvador
👥 6 881 000
✉ 21 041 (8 124)

EQUATORIAL GUINEA, AFRICA
🏢 Malabo
👥 504 000
✉ 28 051 (10 831)

ERITREA, AFRICA
🏢 Asmara
👥 4 401 000
✉ 117 400 (45 328)

ESTONIA, EUROPE
🏢 Tallinn
👥 1 330 000
✉ 45 200 (17 452)

ETHIOPIA, AFRICA
🏢 Addis Ababa
👥 77 431 000
✉ 1 133 880 (437 794)

FINLAND, EUROPE
🏢 Helsinki
👥 5 249 000
✉ 338 145 (130 559)

FRANCE, EUROPE
🏢 Paris
👥 60 496 000
✉ 543 965 (210 026)

GABON, AFRICA
🏢 Libreville
👥 1 384 000
✉ 267 667 (103 347)

GEORGIA, ASIA
🏢 T'bilisi
👥 4 474 000
✉ 69 700 (26 911)

GERMANY, EUROPE
🏢 Berlin
👥 82 689 000
✉ 357 022 (137 849)

GHANA, AFRICA
🏢 Accra
👥 22 113 000
✉ 238 537 (92 100)

GREECE, EUROPE
🏢 Athens
👥 11 120 000
✉ 131 957 (50 949)

GUATEMALA, NORTH AMERICA
🏢 Guatemala City
👥 12 599 000
✉ 108 890 (42 043)

GUINEA, AFRICA
🏢 Conakry
👥 6 402 000
✉ 245 857 (94 926)

GUINEA-BISSAU, AFRICA
🏢 Bissau
👥 1 586 000
✉ 36 125 (13 948)

GUYANA, SOUTH AMERICA
🏢 Georgetown
👥 751 000
✉ 214 969 (83 000)

HAITI, NORTH AMERICA
🏢 Port-au-Prince
👥 8 528 000
✉ 27 750 (10 714)

HONDURAS, NORTH AMERICA
🏢 Tegucigalpa
👥 7 205 000
✉ 112 088 (43 277)

HUNGARY, EUROPE
🏢 Budapest
👥 10 098 000
✉ 93 030 (35 919)

ICELAND, EUROPE
🏢 Reykjavik
👥 295 000
✉ 102 820 (39 699)

INDIA, ASIA
🏢 New Delhi
👥 1 103 371 000
✉ 3 064 898 (1 183 364)

INDONESIA, ASIA
🏢 Jakarta
👥 222 781 000
✉ 1 919 445 (741 102)

IRAN, ASIA
🏢 Tehran
👥 69 515 000
✉ 1 648 000 (636 296)

IRAQ, ASIA
🏢 Baghdad
👥 28 807 000
✉ 438 317 (169 235)

IRELAND EUROPE
🏢 Dublin
👥 4 148 000
✉ 70 282 (27 136)

ISRAEL, ASIA
🏢 Jerusalem
👥 6 725 000
✉ 20 770 (8 019)

ITALY, EUROPE
🏢 Rome
👥 58 093 000
✉ 301 245 (116 311)

JAMAICA, NORTH AMERICA
🏢 Kingston
👥 2 651 000
✉ 10 991 (4 244)

JAPAN, ASIA
🏢 Tokyo
👥 128 085 000
✉ 377 727 (145 841)

JORDAN, ASIA
🏢 Amman
👥 5 703 000
✉ 89 206 (34 443)

KAZAKHSTAN, ASIA
🏢 Astana
👥 14 825 000
✉ 2 717 300 (1 049 155)

KENYA, AFRICA
🏢 Nairobi
👥 34 256 000
✉ 582 646 (224 961)

KUWAIT, ASIA
🏢 Kuwait
👥 2 687 000
✉ 17 818 (6 880)

KYRGYZSTAN, ASIA
🏢 Bishkek
👥 5 264 000
✉ 198 500 (76 641)

LAOS, ASIA
🏢 Vientiane
👥 5 924 000
✉ 236 800 (91 429)

Countries of the World

Country	Capital	Population	Area km² (sq mi)
LATVIA, EUROPE	Riga	2 307 000	63 700 (24 595)
LEBANON, ASIA	Beirut	3 577 000	10 452 (4 036)
LESOTHO, AFRICA	Maseru	1 795 000	30 355 (11 720)
LIBERIA, AFRICA	Monrovia	3 283 000	111 369 (43 000)
LIBYA, AFRICA	Tripoli	5 853 000	1 759 540 (679 362)
LITHUANIA, EUROPE	Vilnius	3 431 000	65 200 (25 174)
LUXEMBOURG, EUROPE	Luxembourg	465 000	2 586 (998)
MACEDONIA, EUROPE	Skopje	2 034 000	25 713 (9 928)
MADAGASCAR, AFRICA	Antananarivo	18 606 000	587 041 (226 658)
MALAWI, AFRICA	Lilongwe	12 884 000	118 484 (45 747)
MALAYSIA, ASIA	Kuala Lumpur/Putrajaya	25 347 000	332 965 (128 559)
MALI, AFRICA	Bamako	13 518 000	1 240 140 (478 821)
MAURITANIA, AFRICA	Nouakchott	3 069 000	1 030 700 (397 955)
MEXICO, NORTH AMERICA	Mexico City	107 029 000	1 972 545 (761 604)
MONGOLIA, ASIA	Ulan Bator	2 646 000	1 565 000 (604 250)
MONTENEGRO, EUROPE	Podgorica	620 000	13 812 (5333)
MOROCCO, AFRICA	Rabat	31 478 000	446 550 (172 414)
MOZAMBIQUE, AFRICA	Maputo	19 792 000	799 380 (308 642)
MYANMAR (BURMA), ASIA	Naypyidaw/Yangon	50 519 000	676 577 (261 228)
NAMIBIA, AFRICA	Windhoek	2 031 000	824 292 (318 261)
NEPAL, ASIA	Kathmandu	27 133 000	147 181 (56 827)
NETHERLANDS, EUROPE	Amsterdam/The Hague	16 299 000	41 526 (16 033)
NEW ZEALAND, OCEANIA	Wellington	4 028 000	270 534 (104 454)
NICARAGUA, NORTH AMERICA	Managua	5 487 000	130 000 (50 193)
NIGER, AFRICA	Niamey	13 957 000	1 267 000 (489 191)
NIGERIA, AFRICA	Abuja	131 530 000	923 768 (356 669)
NORTH KOREA, ASIA	Pyongyang	22 488 000	120 538 (46 540)
NORWAY, EUROPE	Oslo	4 620 000	323 878 (125 050)
OMAN, ASIA	Muscat	2 567 000	309 500 (119 499)
PAKISTAN, ASIA	Islamabad	157 935 000	803 940 (310 403)
PANAMA, NORTH AMERICA	Panama City	3 232 000	77 082 (29 762)
PAPUA NEW GUINEA, OCEANIA	Port Moresby	5 887 000	462 840 (178 704)
PARAGUAY, SOUTH AMERICA	Asunción	6 158 000	406 752 (157 048)
PERU, SOUTH AMERICA	Lima	27 968 000	1 285 216 (496 225)
PHILIPPINES, ASIA	Manila	83 054 000	300 000 (115 831)
POLAND, EUROPE	Warsaw	38 530 000	312 683 (120 728)
PORTUGAL, EUROPE	Lisbon	10 495 000	88 940 (34 340)
QATAR, ASIA	Doha	813 000	11 437 (4 416)
ROMANIA, EUROPE	Bucharest	21 711 000	237 500 (91 699)
RUSSIAN FEDERATION, EUROPE/ASIA	Moscow	143 202 000	17 075 400 (6 592 849)

Country	Capital	Population	Area (sq mi)
(Riyadh)	Riyadh	24 573 000	2 200 000 (849 425)
SENEGAL, AFRICA	Dakar	11 658 000	196 720 (75 954)
SERBIA, EUROPE	Belgrade	9 379 000	88 361 (34 116)
SIERRA LEONE, AFRICA	Freetown	5 525 000	71 740 (27 699)
SINGAPORE, ASIA	Singapore	4 326 000	639 (247)
SLOVAKIA, EUROPE	Bratislava	5 401 000	49 035 (18 933)
SLOVENIA, EUROPE	Ljubljana	1 967 000	20 251 (7 819)
SOMALIA, AFRICA	Mogadishu	8 228 000	637 657 (246 201)
SOUTH AFRICA, REPUBLIC OF AFRICA	Pretoria/Cape Town	47 432 000	1 219 090 (470 693)
SOUTH KOREA, ASIA	Seoul	47 817 000	99 274 (38 330)
SPAIN, EUROPE	Madrid	43 064 000	504 782 (194 897)
SRI LANKA, ASIA	Sri Jayewardenepura Kotte	20 743 000	65 610 (25 332)
SUDAN, AFRICA	Khartoum	36 233 000	2 505 813 (967 500)
SURINAME, SOUTH AMERICA	Paramaribo	449 000	163 820 (63 251)
SWAZILAND, AFRICA	Mbabane	1 032 000	17 364 (6 704)
SWEDEN, EUROPE	Stockholm	9 041 000	449 964 (173 732)
SWITZERLAND, EUROPE	Bern	7 252 000	41 293 (15 943)
SYRIA, ASIA	Damascus	19 043 000	185 180 (71 498)
TAIWAN, ASIA	T'aipei	22 858 000	36 179 (13 969)
TAJIKISTAN, ASIA	Dushanbe	6 507 000	143 100 (55 251)
(Dodoma)	Dodoma	38 329 000	945 087 (364 900)
THAILAND, ASIA	Bangkok	64 233 000	513 115 (198 115)
THE GAMBIA, AFRICA	Banjul	1 517 000	11 295 (4 361)
TOGO, AFRICA	Lomé	6 145 000	56 785 (21 925)
TRINIDAD AND TOBAGO, NORTH AMERICA	Port of Spain	1 305 000	5 130 (1 981)
TUNISIA, AFRICA	Tunis	10 102 000	164 150 (63 379)
TURKEY, ASIA/EUROPE	Ankara	73 193 000	779 452 (300 948)
TURKMENISTAN, ASIA	Ashgabat	4 833 000	488 100 (188 456)
UGANDA, AFRICA	Kampala	28 816 000	241 038 (93 065)
UKRAINE, EUROPE	Kiev	46 481 000	603 700 (233 090)
UNITED ARAB EMIRATES, ASIA	Abu Dhabi	4 496 000	77 700 (30 000)
UNITED KINGDOM, EUROPE	London	59 668 000	243 609 (94 058)
UNITED STATES OF AMERICA, NORTH AMERICA	Washington	298 213 000	9 826 635 (3 794 085)
URUGUAY, SOUTH AMERICA	Montevideo	3 463 000	176 215 (68 037)
UZBEKISTAN, ASIA	Tashkent	26 593 000	447 400 (172 742)
VENEZUELA, SOUTH AMERICA	Caracas	26 749 000	912 050 (352 144)
VIETNAM, ASIA	Hanoi	84 238 000	329 565 (127 246)
YEMEN, ASIA	San'a	20 975 000	527 968 (203 850)
ZAMBIA, AFRICA	Lusaka	11 668 000	752 614 (290 586)
ZIMBABWE, AFRICA	Harare	13 010 000	390 759 (150 873)

Match the numbers on the map to the continent names listed.

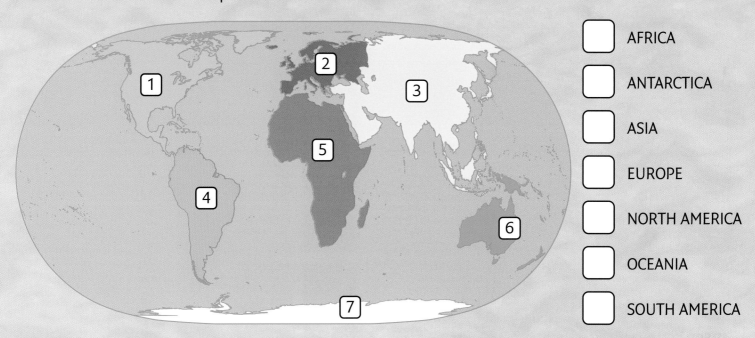

AFRICA

ANTARCTICA

ASIA

EUROPE

NORTH AMERICA

OCEANIA

SOUTH AMERICA

Name the countries

Match the shapes to the country names listed.

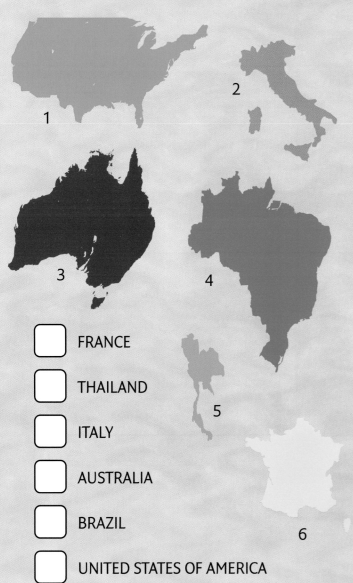

FRANCE

THAILAND

ITALY

AUSTRALIA

BRAZIL

UNITED STATES OF AMERICA

Search for cities

The 12 capital cities listed below are hidden in this grid. See how many you can find.

A	O	W	E	L	L	I	N	G	T	O	N
B	P	X	Z	P	O	J	X	Z	Q	J	O
W	A	S	H	I	N	G	T	O	N	V	T
X	R	K	Y	Y	D	W	V	J	F	X	T
C	I	K	P	F	O	X	Z	Q	J	F	A
A	S	Z	B	A	N	G	K	O	K	X	W
N	J	V	Q	Z	X	X	C	H	Z	Y	A
B	R	A	S	I	L	I	A	W	X	T	V
E	W	H	G	M	X	Z	I	Z	F	U	X
R	O	M	E	X	Q	V	R	J	Q	N	F
R	V	W	T	O	K	Y	O	V	W	I	Q
A	Q	W	H	G	M	X	T	J	V	S	Q

LONDON   WELLINGTON   CAIRO
PARIS   TOKYO   TUNIS
ROME   BANGKOK   OTTAWA
CANBERRA   BRASILIA   WASHINGTON

Quiz 1

1. What is the largest country in the world?

2. What is the capital of France?

3. What colour is the flag of Libya?

Colour match

All these symbols have a colour in part of their name. Find their correct name by matching a colour with one of the other words.

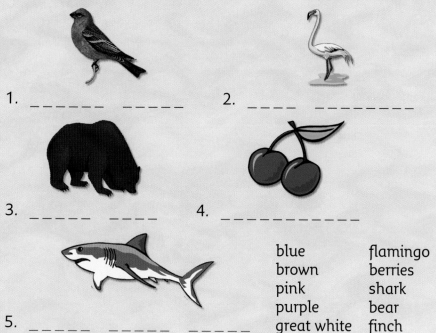

1. _ _ _ _ _ _   _ _ _ _ _

2. _ _ _ _   _ _ _ _ _ _ _ _

3. _ _ _ _ _   _ _ _ _

4. _ _ _ _ _ _ _ _ _ _ _

5. _ _ _ _ _ _   _ _ _ _ _   _ _ _ _ _

blue	flamingo
brown	berries
pink	shark
purple	bear
great white	finch

Unscramble the countries

Rearrange the letters in the boxes to find the names of 6 countries.

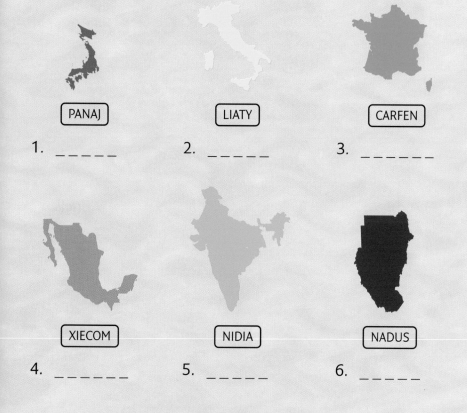

PANAJ

1. _ _ _ _ _

LIATY

2. _ _ _ _ _

CARFEN

3. _ _ _ _ _ _

XIECOM

4. _ _ _ _ _ _

NIDIA

5. _ _ _ _ _

NADUS

6. _ _ _ _ _

Quiz 2

1. What is the world's longest river?

2. How many colours are on the flag of Italy?

3. What kind of bears are found in Arctic regions?

Whose flag is this?

There are 16 country flags and 16 country names shown below. Try to match up the country names to their flag. Add the correct flag number to the box beside each country name.

1. 2.
3. 4.
5. 6.
7. 8.
9. 10.
11. 12.
13. 14.
15. 16.

☐ CHINA   ☐ JAPAN

☐ CANADA   ☐ GREECE

☐ PAKISTAN   ☐ NEPAL

☐ BRAZIL   ☐ SOMALIA

☐ CHILE   ☐ SWEDEN

☐ AUSTRALIA   ☐ KENYA

☐ NEW ZEALAND

☐ UNITED KINGDOM

☐ REPUBLIC OF SOUTH AFRICA

☐ UNITED STATES OF AMERICA

Answers on page 64.

Games and Quizzes

Name the oceans

Match the numbers on the map to the ocean names listed.

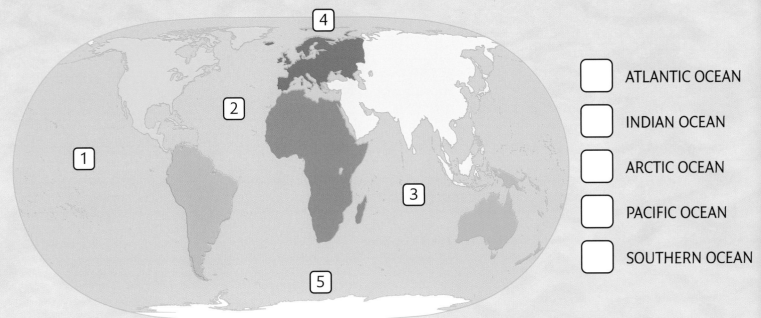

☐ ATLANTIC OCEAN

☐ INDIAN OCEAN

☐ ARCTIC OCEAN

☐ PACIFIC OCEAN

☐ SOUTHERN OCEAN

Name the symbol

Choose a suitable caption for each symbol from the names in the panel on the right.
Only one caption will match each symbol.

Puffin Kiwi fruit Owl	
Bobcat Polar bear	
Grapes Taj Mahal	
Stonehenge Hockey Apple	
Banana Cricket	
Walrus	
Shamrock	
Oil platform	
Sydney Opera House	

1. _____

2. _____

3. _____

4. _____

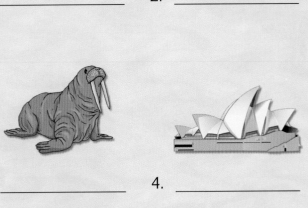

5. _____

6. _____

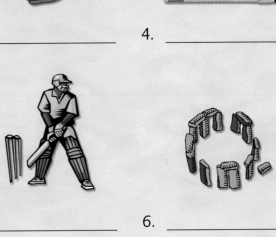

Quiz 3

1. What is the capital of Argentina?

2. How many blue stripes appear on the flag of Honduras?

3. In which country would you watch this sport?

58

Symbol Match

In which country would you expect to see these?
Add the correct symbol number to the box beside each country name.

1. Tower Bridge

2. Croissants

3. Liberty Bell

4. Taj Mahal

5. Kangaroo

6. Zulu house

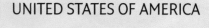 UNITED STATES OF AMERICA   FRANCE

 UNITED KINGDOM   SWAZILAND

 INDIA   AUSTRALIA

Which continent are you in?

Look at the groups of flags below.
Which continent would you be in if these flags were shown?

1.    2.

3. 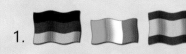   4.

5.    6.

 ASIA   OCEANIA

 EUROPE   NORTH AMERICA

SOUTH AMERICA   AFRICA

Search for countries

The 10 countries listed below
are hidden in this grid.
See how many you can find.

A	R	G	E	N	T	I	N	A	F	K	Y
N	V	G	F	Y	N	E	Z	U	Z	B	V
C	Y	D	Q	C	G	G	G	S	X	Q	J
H	U	N	G	A	R	Y	B	T	G	B	J
I	L	A	F	N	G	P	H	R	B	O	Q
N	N	L	Z	A	S	T	V	A	P	T	X
A	G	O	X	D	T	V	F	L	H	S	F
H	P	O	L	A	N	D	Z	I	H	W	F
H	Y	X	Q	Q	V	Z	X	A	Z	A	O
M	E	X	I	C	O	G	G	V	G	N	Q
Q	Z	J	B	Y	F	F	B	X	B	A	J
N	I	G	E	R	I	A	B	J	Q	K	P

ARGENTINA

AUSTRALIA

BOTSWANA

CANADA

CHINA

EGYPT

HUNGARY

MEXICO

NIGERIA

POLAND

Quiz 4

1. What is the world's highest mountain?

2. What is the capital of China?

3. In which country would you find these animals?

Answers on page 64.

Index

This index lists all the important place names shown on the maps. The grid code numbers and letters help you to find the correct position of the name on each map.

A

Aberdeen 24 C5
Abu Dhabi 35 D2
Abuja 18 C2
Accra 18 C2
Aconcagua 15 B4
Addis Ababa 19 F2
Adelaide 44 B2
Adriatic Sea 29 D3
Afghanistan 35 E4
Africa 16-17
Ahmadabad 37 B4
Alaska 4 A4
Albania 29 D3
Algeria 18 C4
Algiers 18 C5
Alps 28 C4
Amazon 13 D2
Amazon Basin 12 B2
Amman 34 B4
Amsterdam 26 C2
Amudar'ya 35 E4
Andes 12 A1
Andorra 28 B3
Angel Falls 12 C3
Angola 20 B4
Anguilla 9 F3
Ankara 34 B5
Antananarivo 21 D4
Antarctica 47
Antigua and Barbuda 9 F3
Apennines 28 C3
Apia 45 F4
Appalachian Mountains 7 D3
Arabian Sea 36 A3
Aral Sea 35 E5
Archangel 32 B4
Arctic Ocean 46
Argentina 15 B2
Armenia 34 C5
Aruba 9 E2
Asia 30-31
Ashgabat 35 E4
Asmara 19 F3
Astana 32 B2
Asunción 14 C5
Atacama Desert 14 A6
Athens 29 E2
Atlanta 7 D2
Atlantic Ocean 9 F5
Atlas Mountains 18 B4
Auckland 45 E2
Australia 44 B3
Austria 28 C4
Azerbaijan 35 D5

B

Baghdad 34 C4
Bahrain 35 D3
Baku 35 D5
Balearic Islands 28 B3
Baltic Sea 27 D2

Bamako 18 B3
Bandar Seri Begawan 40 C3
Bangkok 40 A4
Bangladesh 36 D4
Bangui 20 B6
Banjul 18 B3
Barbados 9 F2
Barcelona 28 B3
Barents Sea 32 B4
Barquisimeto 12 B4
Barranquilla 12 B4
Bay of Bengal 37 D3
Bay of Biscay 28 B4
Beijing 38 C3
Beirut 34 B4
Belém 13 E2
Belarus 27 E2
Belfast 25 B4
Belgium 26 C2
Belgrade 29 D3
Belize 8 C3
Belmopan 8 C3
Belo Horizonte 14 D5
Ben Nevis 24 B5
Benin 18 C2
Bering Sea 33 E5
Berlin 27 D2
Bern 28 C4
Bhutan 36 D5
Birmingham 25 C2
Bishkek 32 B1
Bissau 18 B3
Black Sea 34 B5
Bogotá 12 B3
Bolivia 14 B6
Borneo 40 C2
Bosnia-Herzegovina 29 D3
Boston 7 E4
Botswana 21 B3
Brasília 14 D6
Bratislava 29 D4
Brazil 14 C6
Brazilian Highlands 14 D6
Brazzaville 20 B5
Brisbane 44 C3
Bristol 25 C2
Brunei 40 C3
Brussels 26 C2
Bucharest 29 E3
Budapest 27 D1
Buenos Aires 15 B4
Bujumbura 20 C5
Bulgaria 29 E3
Burkina 18 C3
Burundi 20 C5

C

Cairo 19 E4
Calgary 4 B2
Cambodia 40 B4
Cambrian Mountains 25 C2
Cameroon 19 D2
Campinas 14 D5

Canada 4 C3
Canary Islands 18 B4
Canberra 44 C2
Cape Town 21 B2
Cape Verde 18 A3
Caracas 12 C4
Cardiff 25 C2
Caribbean Sea 9 D3
Carpathian Mountains 27 E1
Cartagena 12 B4
Casablanca 18 B4
Caspian Sea 35 D5
Cayenne 13 D3
Central African Republic
  20 B6
Chad 19 D3
Chang Jiang 38 C2
Chelyabinsk 32 B2
Chennai 37 C2
Chicago 7 D4
Chile 15 A2
China 38 B3
Chisinau 29 E4
Chittagong 37 D4
Chongqing 38 C2
Cincinnati 7 D3
Cologne 28 C4
Colombia 12 B3
Colorado 6 B3
Comoros 20 D4
Conakry 18 B2
Congo 20 B5
Congo 20 B6
Congo Basin 20 B5
Copenhagen 27 D2
Coral Sea 44 C4
Cork 25 A2
Costa Rica 9 D2
Côte d'Ivoire 18 B2
Croatia 29 D3
Cuba 9 D3
Curitiba 14 C5
Cyprus 34 B4
Czech Republic 27 D1

D

Dakar 18 B3
Dallas 6 C2
Damascus 34 C4
Danube 29 D3
Dar es Salaam 20 D5
Darling 44 C2
Darwin 44 B4
Deccan 37 B3
Delhi 36 B5
Democratic Republic of the
  Congo 20 B6
Denmark 26 C3
Denver 6 B3
Detroit 7 D4
Dhaka 37 D4
Dili 41 D1
Djibouti 19 F3

Djibouti (city) 19 F3
Dnieper 27 E2
Dodoma 20 C5
Doha 35 D3
Dominica 9 F3
Dominican Republic 9 E3
Drakensberg 21 C2
Dublin 25 B3
Dundee 24 C5
Durban 21 C3
Dushanbe 35 F4

E

East China Sea 39 D2
East Siberian Sea 33 D5
East Timor 41 D1
Eastern Ghats 37 C2
Ecuador 12 A2
Edinburgh 24 C4
Egypt 19 E4
Elbe 27 D2
El'brus 34 C5
El Salvador 8 C2
England 25 C3
English Channel 25 D1
Equatorial Guinea 18 C2
Eritrea 19 E3
Estonia 27 E3
Europe 22-23
Ethiopia 19 E2
Ethiopian Highlands 19 E2

F

Faisalabad 36 B5
Falkland Islands 15 B1
Faroe Islands 26 B4
Federated States of
  Micronesia 30 C5
Fiji 45 E3
Finland 27 E4
Firth of Forth 24 C4
Fortaleza 13 F2
France 28 B4
Frankfurt 28 C4
Freetown 18 B2
French Guiana 13 D3

G

Gabon 20 A5
Gaborone 21 B3
Galway 25 A3
Ganges 36 C4
Georgetown 13 D4
Georgia 34 C5
Germany 26 C2
Ghana 18 C2
Glasgow 24 C4
Gobi Desert 38 B4
Godavari 37 C3
Goiânia 14 C6
Grampian Mountains 24 C5

Gran Chaco 14 B5
Great Australian Bight
  44 B2
Great Barrier Reef 44 C4
Great Dividing Range 44 C3
Great Rift Valley 20 C5
Great Sandy Desert 44 A3
Great Victoria Desert 44 B2
Greece 29 D2
Greenland 5 D5
Grenada 9 F2
Guadalajara 8 B3
Guadeloupe 9 F3
Guatemala 8 C2
Guatemala City 8 C2
Guayaquil 12 A2
Guiana Highlands 12 C3
Guinea 18 B2
Guinea Bissau 18 B3
Gulf of Aden 19 F3
Gulf of Alaska 4 A4
Gulf of California 8 A5
Gulf of Guinea 18 C2
Gulf of Mexico 8 C4
Gulf of Oman 34 C1
Guyana 12 C3

H

Haiti 9 E3
Hamburg 28 C5
Hannover 28 C5
Hanoi 40 B5
Harare 21 C4
Havana 9 D3
Helsinki 27 E3
Himalaya 36 B5
Hindu Kush 35 F4
Honduras 8 C2
Hong Kong 38 C1
Honiara 45 D4
Houston 6 C2
Hudson Bay 5 D2
Hungary 27 D1
Hyderabad 37 B3

I

Iceland 26 B5
India 37 B4
Indian Ocean 20 D5
Indonesia 40 C2
Indore 37 B4
Indus 35 F4
Inverness 24 C5
Iguacu Falls 14 C5
Iran 35 D4
Iraq 34 C3
Ireland 25 A3
Irish Sea 25 B3
Irkutsk 33 D2
Irrawaddy 37 D3
Irtysh 32 B2
Islamabad 36 B5
Isle of Man 25 B3
Israel 34 B4
Istanbul 29 E3
Italy 28 C3

J

Jaipur 36 B4
Jakarta 40 B2
Jamaica 9 D3
Japan 39 D4
Java 40 B2
Java Sea 40 B2
Jerusalem 34 B4
Johannesburg 21 C3
Jordan 34 C4

K

K2 38 A3
Kabul 35 F4
Kalahari Desert 21 B3
Kamchatka Peninsula 33 E4
Kampala 20 C5
Kansas City 6 C3
Karachi 37 A4
Karakoram Range 35 F4
Kathmandu 36 C5
Kazakhstan 32 B2
Kenya 20 C6
Khabarovsk 33 E2
Khartoum 19 E3
Kiev 29 E5
Kigali 20 C5
Kilimanjaro 20 C5
Kingston 9 D3
Kinshasa 20 B5
Kiribati 45 E5
Kolkata 37 D4
Krasnoyarsk 32 C2
Kuala Lumpur 40 B3
Kunlun Shan 38 A3
Kuwait 35 D3
Kuwait (city) 35 D3
Kyrgyzstan 32 B1

L

Laayoune 18 B4
Lagos 18 C2
Lahore 36 B5
Lake Baikal 33 D2
Lake Balkhash 32 B2
Lake Chad 19 D3
Lake Erie 7 D4
Lake Huron 7 D4
Lake Lagoda 27 E4
Lake Michigan 7 D4
Lake Nicaragua 9 D2
Lake Nyasa 20 C4
Lake Onega 27 E4
Lake Ontario 7 E4
Lake Superior 7 D4
Lake Tanganyika 20 C5
Lake Titicaca 14 A6
Lake Turkana 20 C6
Lake Victoria 20 C5
Laos 40 B5
La Paz 14 A6
Lappland 27 D5
Las Vegas 6 A3
Latvia 27 E3
Lebanon 34 B4
Leeds 25 C3

Lena 33 D3
Lesotho 21 C3
Liberia 18 B2
Libreville 20 A5
Libya 19 D4
Liechtenstein 28 C4
Lilongwe 20 C4
Lima 12 A1
Limerick 25 A3
Limpopo 21 C3
Lisbon 28 A3
Lithuania 27 E2
Liverpool 25 C3
Ljubljana 29 D4
Lomé 18 C2
London 25 D2
Londonderry 25 B4
Los Angeles 6 A3
Lough Neagh 25 B4
Luanda 20 A5
Lubumbashi 20 C4
Lusaka 21 C4
Luxembourg 26 C1
Luxembourg (city) 26 C1
Luzon 40 D5

M

Macedonia 29 D3
Madagascar 21 D3
Madeira 12 C2
Madrid 28 B3
Malabo 18 C2
Malawi 20 C4
Malaysia 40 B3
Maldives 37 B1
Mali 18 C3
Malta 29 D2
Managua 9 D2
Manama 35 D3
Manaus 12 C2
Manchester 25 C3
Mandalay 37 D4
Manila 40 C4
Maputo 21 C3
Maracaibo 12 B4
Marseille 28 C3
Martinique 9 F3
Maseru 21 C3
Massif Central 28 B4
Mauritania 18 B3
Mauritius 17 D3
Mbabane 21 C3
Medellín 12 B3
Mediterranean Sea 28 C2
Melbourne 44 C2
Melekeok 41 E3
Mendoza 15 B4
Mexico 8 B4
Mexico City 8 B3
Miami 7 E1
Middlesbrough 24 C4
Milan 28 C3
Mindanao 41 D3
Minneapolis 6 C4
Minsk 27 E2
Missouri 6 B5
Mogadishu 20 D6
Moldova 29 E4
Monaco 28 C3

Mongolia 38 B4
Monrovia 18 B2
Montenegro 29 D3
Monterrey 8 B4
Montevideo 15 C3
Montréal 5 D1
Montserrat 9 F3
Morocco 18 B4
Moscow 32 A3
Mount Everest 36 C4
Mount Logan 4 B3
Mount McKinley 4 A4
Mount Rainer 6 A4
Mozambique 21 C3
Mumbai 37 B3
Munich 28 C4
Murray 44 C2
Muscat 35 E2
Myanmar (Burma) 40 A5

N

Nagpur 37 C3
Nairobi 20 C5
Namib Desert 21 B3
Namibia 21 B4
Nassau 9 D4
Nauru 45 D5
Naypyidaw 40 A5
Ndjamena 19 D2
Negro 12 C3
Nepal 36 C5
Netherlands 26 C2
New Caledonia 45 D3
Newcastle upon Tyne
  25 C4
New Delhi 36 B5
New Guinea 41 E2
New Orleans 7 D2
New York 7 E4
New Zealand 45 E1
Niagara Falls 5 D1
Niamey 18 C3
Nicaragua 9 D2
Nicosia 34 B4
Niger 18 C3
Nigeria 18 C2
Nile 19 E4
North America 2-3
Northern Ireland 25 B4
North Korea 39 D4
North Sea 24 C4
Norway 26 C3
Nouakchott 18 B3
Nouméa 45 D3
Novosibirsk 32 C2
Nuku'alofa 45 F3
Nuuk (Godthåb) 5 E3

O

Ob 32 B3
Oceania 42 -43
Oman 35 D2
Omsk 32 B2
Oporto 28 A3
Orange 21 B3
Orinoco 12 C4
Orkney Islands 24 C6
Oslo 27 D3

Ottawa 5 D1
Ougadougou 18 C3
Outer Hebrides 24 B5

P

Pacific Ocean 4 A3
Pakistan 35 E3
Palau 41 E3
Panama 9 D2
Panama Canal 9 D2
Panama City 9 D2
Papua New Guinea 44 C5
Paraguay 14 B5
Paramaribo 13 D3
Paraná 14 C5
Paris 28 B4
Patagonia 15 A1
Patna 36 C4
Pechora 32 B4
Perm 32 B3
Perth 44 A2
Peru 12 B1
Philadelphia 7 E3
Philippines 41 D4
Phnom Penh 40 B4
Phoenix 6 B2
Pittsburgh 7 E3
Planalto do Mato Grosso
  14 C7
Plateau of Tibet 38 A3
Po 28 C3
Podgorica 29 D3
Poland 27 D2
Port-au-Prince 9 E3
Port Moresby 44 C4
Porto Alegre 14 C4
Porto-Novo 18 C2
Portsmouth 25 C1
Portugal 28 A3
Port Vila 45 E3
Prague 27 D1
Praia 18 A3
Pretoria (Tshwane) 21 C3
Puerto Rico 9 F3
Puncak Jaya 41 E2
Putrajaya 40 B3
Pyongyang 39 D4
Pyrenees 28 B3

Q

Qatar 35 D3
Québec 5 E1
Quito 12 A3

R

Rabat 18 C5
Ras Dejen 19 F3
Recife 13 F1
Red Sea 19 E4
Republic of South Africa
  21 B3
Reykjavík 26 B5
Rhône 28 C3
Rhine 26 C2
Riga 27 E3
Rio de Janeiro 14 D5
Rio Grande 8 B4

Riyadh 34 C3
Rocky Mountains 4 B4
Romania 29 D4
Rome 28 C3
Rosario 15 B4
Russian Federation 32 C3
Rwanda 20 C5

S

Sahara 18 C4
St George's Channel 25 B2
St Kitts and Nevis 9 F3
St Lawrence 5 E2
St Louis 7 D3
St Lucia 9 F2
St Petersburg 27 E3
St Vincent and the
  Grenadines 9 F2
Sakhalin 33 E3
Salvador 13 F1
Samoa 45 F4
San'a 34 C1
San Diego 6 A3
San Francisco 6 A3
San José 9 D2
San Juan 9 F3
San Marino 28 C3
San Salvador 8 C2
Santa Cruz 14 B6
Santiago 15 A4
Santo Domingo 9 E3
Santos 14 D5
São Francisco 13 F1
São Paulo 14 D5
São Tomé 18 C2
São Tomé and Principe 18 C2
Sapporo 39 E4
Sarajevo 29 D3
Sardinia 28 C3
Saudi Arabia 34 C2
Scotland 24 B5
Sea of Japan (East Sea)
  39 D4
Sea of Okhotsk 33 E3
Seattle 6 A5
Seine 26 C1
Senegal 18 B3
Seoul 39 D3
Serbia 29 D3
Seychelles 17 D4
Shanghai 39 D2
Shannon 25 A3
Sheffield 25 C3
Shetland Islands 24 C7
Siberia 32 C3
Sicily 28 C2
Sierra Leone 18 B2
Singapore 40 B3
Singapore 40 B3
Skopje 29 D3
Slovakia 29 D4
Slovenia 29 D4
Sofia 29 D3
Solomon Islands 45 D4
Solway Firth 25 C4
Somalia 20 D6
South America 10–11
Southampton 25 C1
South China Sea 38 C1

Southern Ocean 47
South Korea 39 D3
Spain 28 A3
Sri Jayewardenepura Kotte
  37 C1
Sri Lanka 37 C1
Stockholm 27 D3
Stoke-on-Trent 25 C3
Strait of Gibraltar 28 A2
Sucre 14 B6
Sudan 19 E3
Suez Canal 19 E4
Sumatra 40 B2
Suriname 13 D3
Suva 45 E3
Swansea 25 C2
Swaziland 21 C3
Sweden 27 D3
Switzerland 28 C4
Sydney 44 C2
Syria 34 C4
Syrian Desert 34 C4

T

Tagus 28 A3
T'aipei 39 D2
Taiwan 39 D1
Tajikistan 35 F4
Tallinn 27 E3
Tanzania 20 C5
Tashkent 35 F5
Tasman Sea 45 D1
Taurus Mountains 34 B4
T'bilisi 35 D5
Tegucigalpa 8 C2
Tehran 35 D4
Thailand 40 B4
Thar Desert 36 B4
The Bahamas 9 E4
The Gambia 18 B3
The Gulf 35 D3
The Hague 26 C2
The Pennines 25 C3
Thimphu 36 D5
Tien Shan 38 A4
Tierra del Fuego 15 B1
Timor Sea 44 A4
Tirana 29 D3
Tocantins 13 E1
Togo 18 C2
Tokyo 39 E3
Tonga 45 F3
Toronto 5 D1
Trent 25 D3
Trinidad and Tobago 9 F2
Tripoli 19 D4
Tunis 19 D5
Tunisia 18 C4
Turkey 34 C4
Turkmenistan 35 D4
Turks and Caicos Islands 9 E3
Tuvalu 45 E4
Tyne 25 C4

U

Uganda 20 C6
Ukraine 29 E4
Ulan Bator 38 C4

Uluru (Ayers Rock) 44 B3
United Arab Emirates 35 D2
United Kingdom 25 B4
United States of America
  6 B3
Ural Mountains 32 B3
Uruguay 15 C4
Uzbekistan 35 E5

V

Valletta 29 D2
Vancouver 4 B2
Vanuatu 45 D4
Venezuela 12 C4
Victoria Falls 21 C4
Vienna 29 D4
Vientiane 40 B5
Vietnam 40 B4
Vilnius 27 E2
Vistula 27 D2
Vladivostok 33 E2
Volgograd 32 A3

W

Wales 25 C2
Warsaw 27 D2
Washington D.C. 7 E3
Wellington 45 E1
Western Ghats 37 B3
Western Sahara 18 B4
Windhoek 21 B3
Winnipeg 4 C2
Wrangel Island 33 E5

X

Xi'an 38 C3

Y

Yamoussoukro 18 B2
Yangon (Rangoon) 40 A4
Yaoundé 19 D2
Yaren 45 D5
Yekaterinburg 32 B3
Yellow Sea 39 D3
Yemen 34 C1
Yenisey 32 C3
Yerevan 34 C5
York 25 C3
Yucatán 8 C3
Yukon 4 B4

Z

Zagreb 29 D4
Zagros Mountains 35 D3
Zambezi 21 C4
Zambia 20 B4
Zimbabwe 21 C4

	Try this!	**What am I?**
2-3	GREENLAND	
4-5	1. Canadian goose, Arctic tern, snowy owl, snow goose, ptarmigan 2. Newfoundland, husky 3. polar bear, musk ox, Arctic fox, wolf, brown bear, bobcat, caribou, moose, beaver, Arctic hare	A maple leaf
6-7	1. blueberries, grapes, oranges, apples 2. hotdog, hamburger, muffin 3. peanut	A hot dog
8-9	1. tropical fish, sea horse, great white shark, elephant seal, monk seal, turtle 2. parrot, toucan	A cactus
10-11	1. Colombia, Chile 2. Bogota, Brasilia	
12-13	1. emerald, diamond 2. anaconda	A condor
14-15	1. mackerel, sardine 2. polo, skiing, football, motor racing	A killer whale
16-17	MADAGASCAR	
18-19	1. camel, gerbil, baboon 2. scorpion, tortoise 3. hoopoe, hornbill bird, bee eater bird, secretary bird	A camel
20-21	1. grapes, oranges 2. cloves	A sand dune
22-23	1. Two. Germany and Belgium 2. Greece 3. Norway	
24-25	1. football, cricket, rugby 2. yachting, windsurfing 3. curling, skiing	A shamrock
26-27	1. Gouda 2. dairy cows, pigs, sheep 3. croissant	An owl
28-29		Spaghetti
30-31	Sri Lanka	
32-33	1. reindeer, polar bear, Siberian tiger, Siberian husky, Siberian stag, brown bear, lynx, Caspian seal, lemming 2. eider duck, snow goose, Ural owl	A brown bear
34-35	1. Arabian camel, Arabian fox, Arabian horse 2. Mosque 3. cricket	A flamingo
36-37	1. tiger, snow leopard, Asiatic lion 2. peacock, parakeet 3. Indian porcupine	An octopus
38-39	1. Giant panda 2. karate, sumo wrestling, skiing	A terracotta soldier
40-41	1. surfing and scuba diving	A Komodo dragon
42-43	FIJI AUSTRALIA NAURU	
44-45	1. black swan 2. sea horses, sperm whale, barracuda, flying fish, clown fish, great white shark, swordfish, octopus	A kangaroo
46	1. ski plane 2. kayak 3. snowmobile	
47		A penguin

56-57 Games and quizzes

Name the continents
1. North America
2. Europe
3. Asia
4. South America
5. Africa
6. Oceania
7. Antarctica

Name the countries
1. United States of America
2. Italy
3. Australia
4. Brazil
5. Thailand
6. France

Search for cities

A	O	W	E	L	L	I	N	G	T	O	N
B	P	X	Z	P	O	J	X	Z	Q	J	O
W	A	S	H	I	N	G	T	O	N	V	T
X	R	K	Y	Y	D	W	V	J	F	X	T
C	I	K	P	F	O	X	Z	Q	J	F	A
A	S	Z	B	A	N	G	K	O	K	X	W
N	J	V	Q	Z	X	X	C	H	Z	Y	A
B	R	A	S	I	L	I	A	W	X	T	V
E	W	H	G	M	X	Z	I	Z	F	U	X
R	O	M	E	X	Q	V	R	J	Q	N	F
R	V	W	T	O	K	Y	O	V	W	I	Q
A	Q	W	H	G	M	X	T	J	V	S	Q

Quiz 1
1. Russian Federation
2. Paris
3. Green

Colour match
1. purple finch
2. pink flamingo
3. brown bear
4. blueberries
5. great white shark

Unscramble the countries
1. Japan
2. Italy
3. France
4. Mexico
5. India
6. Sudan

Quiz 2
1. River Nile
2. 3 (green, white and red)
3. Polar bears

Whose flag is this?
1. Canada
2. Australia
3. Greece
4. United States of America
5. Pakistan
6. Sweden
7. Brazil
8. Kenya
9. China
10. United Kingdom
11. New Zealand
12. Japan
13. Nepal
14. Chile
15. Republic of South Africa
16. Somalia

58-59 Games and quizzes

Name the oceans
1. Pacific Ocean
2. Atlantic Ocean
3. Indian Ocean
4. Arctic Ocean
5. Southern Ocean

Name the symbol
1. Puffin
2. Kiwi fruit
3. Walrus
4. Sydney Opera House
5. Cricket
6. Stonehenge

Quiz 3
1. Buenos Aires
2. 2
3. Japan

Symbol match
1. United Kingdom
2. France
3. United States of America
4. India
5. Australia
6. Swaziland

Which continent are you in?
1. Europe
2. Africa
3. North America
4. Asia
5. Oceania
6. South America

Search for countries

A	R	G	E	N	T	I	N	A	F	K	Y
N	V	G	F	Y	N	E	Z	U	Z	B	V
C	Y	D	Q	C	G	G	G	S	X	Q	J
H	U	N	G	A	R	Y	B	T	G	B	J
I	L	A	F	N	G	P	H	R	B	O	Q
N	N	L	Z	A	S	T	V	A	P	T	X
A	G	O	X	D	T	V	F	L	H	S	F
H	P	O	L	A	N	D	Z	I	H	W	F
H	Y	X	Q	Q	V	Z	X	A	Z	A	O
M	E	X	I	C	O	G	G	V	G	N	Q
Q	Z	J	B	Y	F	F	B	X	B	A	J
N	I	G	E	R	I	A	B	J	Q	K	P

Quiz 4
1. Mount Everest
2. Beijing
3. Australia